THIS BOOK BELONGS TO

_____

START DATE

_____

SHE READS TRUTH

EXECUTIVE

FOUNDER/CHIEF EXECUTIVE OFFICER
Raechel Myers

CO-FOUNDER/CHIEF CONTENT OFFICER
Amanda Bible Williams

CHIEF OPERATING OFFICER
Ryan Myers

EXECUTIVE ASSISTANT
Catherine Cromer

EDITORIAL

CONTENT DIRECTOR
John Greco, MDiv

MANAGING EDITOR
Jessica Lamb

CONTENT EDITOR
Kara Gause

ASSOCIATE EDITORS
Bailey Gillespie
Ellen Taylor

CREATIVE

CREATIVE DIRECTOR
Jeremy Mitchell

LEAD DESIGNER
Kelsea Allen

ARTIST IN RESIDENCE
Emily Knapp

DESIGNERS
Abbey Benson
Davis DeLisi

MARKETING

MARKETING DIRECTOR
Casey Campbell

MARKETING MANAGER
Katie Matuska

SOCIAL MEDIA STRATEGIST
Ansley Rushing

PARTNERSHIP SPECIALIST
Kamiren Passavanti

COMMUNITY SUPPORT SPECIALIST
Margot Williams

SHIPPING & LOGISTICS

LOGISTICS MANAGER
Lauren Gloyne

SHIPPING MANAGER
Sydney Bess

FULFILLMENT COORDINATOR
Katy McKnight

FULFILLMENT SPECIALISTS
Sam Campos
Julia Rogers

SUBSCRIPTION INQUIRIES
orders@shereadstruth.com

CONTRIBUTORS

PHOTOGRAPHERS
Erica Griffith (30, 104)
Erin Krespan (54, 78)
Abby Shadle (94)
Kimberly Strunk (126)

RECIPES
Angela Cay Hall,
@seedplantwatergrow (98, 118)
Marilou Perry Woods (88)

WREATH CRAFT
Terri and Ashley Woods,
@field_and_forage (48)

@SHEREADSTRUTH

Download the
She Reads Truth app,
available for iOS
and Android.

SHEREADSTRUTH.COM

This book was printed offset in Nashville, Tennessee, on 70# Lynx Opaque. Cover is 100# Cougar Opaque with Infinity Foil #43 and a soft touch lamination.

Advent 2019

A THRILL OF HOPE

SHE READS TRUTH

Our HOLY GOD INCARNATE
is the THRILL OF HOPE *the*
WORLD *was* WAITING FOR.

Raechel Myers
FOUNDER & CHIEF
EXECUTIVE OFFICER

There is just something about the Advent season.

I love a good set of flannel pajamas, a crackling fire, wassail simmering on the stovetop, and the nothing-like-it glow of the Christmas tree—all while the nostalgic sound of Vince Guaraldi's piano fills the air with memories of Christmases long past, before we were old enough to buy gifts.

The music and the ambiance would be wonderful even if we were experiencing them for the very first time, but what really makes them special—what makes the season really sing—is that *we did it this way last year, too*. Or, because *I remember this smell of spiced cider from when I was a child*. The layering of tradition adorns this season like no other. Even our decorations tell a story. Carefully and expectantly, we lift each ornament out of its packaging, remembering the Christmas it was given to us, or what it looked like hanging from our mother's tree.

This is what I love about traditional Advent scriptures. Like that box of ornaments we pull out of the attic, we unpack the familiar verses, one at a time. Weary world that we are, we read the ancient truth once more—a prophecy first, a promise after that—to remember again why we needed Christmas. Each passage builds on the last, telling a story and adorning our season, building an eagerness within us for the moment we stand at the scene of the nativity and rejoice that this is the night of our dear Savior's birth.

Our holy God incarnate is the thrill of hope the world was waiting for, and He is the One we wait for once again.

Whether you are brand new to the story of Jesus's birth, or you grew up lighting Advent wreaths and reciting Luke 2 from memory, our prayer is that the Scripture in this book would feel like home to you. From the first promise of the Messiah to the moment Jesus is presented in the temple, we pray that you will sense the quiet, unmistakable thrill of hope that is yours because the Son of God became a baby.

There is just something about this season, friends. And we are honored to unpack the Advent story with you.

Merry Christmas!

Advent 2019

A THRILL OF HOPE

LOOK FOR PAPER
QUILLED GREENERY
THROUGHOUT THE
BOOK, TOO!

Paper quilling is an art form rooted in tradition. Dating all the way back to the Renaissance, it is a reflective craft with a pace and process that allow for contemplation and rest. The technique itself is relatively simple to learn, and our team had fun experimenting with different paper types and quilling tools. Our favorite creation is the big, beautiful "A" that adorns the cover of this book.

She Reads Truth is a community of women dedicated to reading the Word of God every day.

The Bible is living and active, breathed out by God, and we confidently hold it higher than anything we can do or say. This book focuses primarily on Scripture, with bonus resources to facilitate deeper engagement with God's Word.

SCRIPTURE READING

Designed to begin on Sunday, December 1, this Study Book presents daily readings for the Advent season.

Look for this icon to learn more about the Christmas story alongside the daily readings!

RESPONSE

Each daily reading features space for personal reflection and prayer.

GRACE DAY

Use Saturdays to pray, rest, and reflect on the advent of Christ.

SUNDAYS OF ADVENT

Each Sunday features a short Scripture passage and reflection based on traditional themes for the four Sundays of Advent and the first Sunday of Christmastide.

Find the corresponding memory cards in the back of this book.

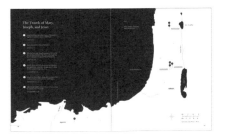

EXTRAS

This book features additional tools to help you gain a deeper understanding of the text.

For added community and
conversation, join us in the
Advent 2019: A Thrill of Hope
reading plan on the She Reads Truth
app or at SheReadsTruth.com.

Table of Contents

71 A GINGERBREAD COTTAGE FOR THE SHES

CANDY CANE DATE BALLS 99

WINTER WASSAIL 29

DECEMBER

2019

Lord, let not our souls be busy inns that have no room for Thee or Thine,
But quiet homes of prayer and praise, where Thou mayest find fit company,
Where the needful cares of life are wisely ordered and put away,
And wide, sweet spaces kept for Thee; where holy thoughts pass up and down
And fervent longings watch and wait Thy coming.

JULIAN OF NORWICH

S	M
ADVENT BEGINS **1**	2
The First Sunday of Advent	Celebrate **Giving Tuesday** with a donation to your favorite charity or cause.
DAY 1 • PAGE 18	DAY 2 • PAGE 22
8	9
The Second Sunday of Advent	Today is the **last day to order** from ShopSheReadsTruth.com for delivery by Christmas with **standard** shipping!
DAY 8 • PAGE 50	DAY 9 • PAGE 55
15	16
The Third Sunday of Advent	DON'T FORGET! Today is the **last day to order** from ShopSheReadsTruth.com for delivery by Christmas with **fast** shipping!
DAY 15 • PAGE 82	DAY 16 • PAGE 85
22	23
The Fourth Sunday of Advent	
DAY 22 • PAGE 112	DAY 23 • PAGE 114
29	30
The First Sunday of Christmastide	
DAY 29 • PAGE 146	

T	W	T	F	S
3	4	5	6	GRACE DAY 7
✂ · · · · · · · · Browse this book to find our **Christmas crafts** and gather the supplies you need for cross-stitching and more!				Use Saturdays to pray, rest, and reflect on the hope we have because Jesus came.
DAY 3 • PAGE 25	DAY 4 • PAGE 31	DAY 5 • PAGE 34	DAY 6 • PAGE 41	DAY 7 • PAGE 47
10	11	12	13	GRACE DAY 14
	Scan this QR code to listen to our **Advent playlist** on Spotify!			
DAY 10 • PAGE 61	DAY 11 • PAGE 64	DAY 12 • PAGE 67	DAY 13 • PAGE 74	DAY 14 • PAGE 79
17	18	19	20	GRACE DAY 21 FIRST DAY OF WINTER
	Make a batch of **cinnamon candy** for a mid-season treat! See recipe on page 89.		Order your **Genesis Study Book** by Monday for delivery in time for the January 6 start date. Discount code on page 157!	
DAY 17 • PAGE 91	DAY 18 • PAGE 95	DAY 19 • PAGE 100	DAY 20 • PAGE 105	DAY 21 • PAGE 109
24	CHRISTMASTIDE BEGINS 25 Christmas Day DAY 25 • PAGE 127	26	27	GRACE DAY 28
DAY 24 • PAGE 120		DAY 26 • PAGE 133	DAY 27 • PAGE 139	DAY 28 • PAGE 145
NEW YEAR'S EVE 31	NEW YEAR'S DAY JAN 1	JAN 2	JAN 3	JAN 4
Turn to **For the Record** on page 150 to reflect on 2019 and pray for the year ahead.				Start your year in the Word. Read **Genesis** with SRT, beginning January 6!

KEY VERSE

I wait for the Lord; I wait
and put my hope in his word.

PSALM 130:5

WHAT IS
Advent?

From ancient times, Christians have anticipated the celebration of Christmas with Advent, a season of hope and expectation. The name *Advent* comes from a Latin word meaning "coming" or "arrival."

As followers of Christ, we are a people living between two advents—the coming of Jesus as a baby to Bethlehem, and His triumphant return as the King of kings at the close of history. So, year after year, from the fourth Sunday before Christmas until Christmas Eve, believers down through the centuries and across the globe have set aside this season to remember and anticipate their King.

A SEASON TO REMEMBER

We remember that our Savior emptied Himself to become one of us, stepping out of eternity to take on flesh. He was born among us to live the righteous life we cannot live. Then He died, the perfect sacrifice on our behalf, so that we could be spared the punishment our sin justly deserves. But the grave could not hold Him, and in His resurrection from the dead, we have the promise of eternal life.

A SEASON TO ANTICIPATE

We anticipate Christ's promised return, when He will one day come again, bringing with Him the fullness of His kingdom. On that day, every tear will be wiped away; there will be no more pain, grief, or death. All things will be made new, and the dwelling place of God will be with His people.

At Christmas, we don't just remember that Jesus came; we celebrate why He came. And as we do, we worship the living Savior who has promised to come again. This is the heart of Advent.

. . .

A Liturgy

to Mark the Start of the Christmas Season

LEADER   As we prepare our house for the coming
         Christmas season, we would also prepare our
         hearts for the returning Christ.

PEOPLE   **You came once for your people,**
         O Lord, and you will come for us again.

         Though there was no room at the inn
         to receive you upon your first arrival
         We would prepare you room
            here in our hearts
            and here in our home,
         Lord Christ.

         As we decorate and celebrate, we do so to mark
         the memory of your redemptive movement into
         our broken world, O God.

         Our glittering ornaments and Christmas trees,
         Our festive carols, our sumptuous feasts—
         By these small tokens we affirm
         that something amazing has happened
         in time and space—
         that God, on a particular night, in a particular
         place, so many years ago, was born to us, an
         infant King, our Prince of Peace.

         Our wreaths and ribbons and colored lights,
         our giving of gifts, our parties with friends—
         these have never been ends in themselves.

They are but small ways in which we repeat
that sounding joy first proclaimed by angels
in the skies near Bethlehem.

In view of such great tidings of love announced
to us, and to all people, how can we not
be moved to praise and celebration in this
Christmas season?
As we decorate our tree, and as we
feast and laugh and sing together,
we are rehearsing our coming joy!
We are making ready to receive the one
who has already, with open arms, received us!
We would prepare you room
   here in our hearts
   and here in our home,
Lord Christ.

Now we celebrate your first coming, Immanuel,
even as we long for your return.
O Prince of Peace, our elder brother, return
soon. We miss you so!

Amen.

—Douglas McKelvey, *Every Moment Holy*

. . .

The First Sunday of Advent

DAY 1

Prophets Sunday

Jesus Christ is the Alpha and Omega of the Bible. He is the
constant theme of its sacred pages; from first to last they testify
of Him. At the creation we at once discern Him as one of the
sacred Trinity; we catch a glimpse of Him in the promise of the
woman's seed; we see Him typified in the ark of Noah; we walk
with Abraham, as He sees Messiah's day; we dwell in the tents
of Isaac and Jacob, feeding upon the gracious promise; we hear
the venerable Israel talking of Shiloh; and in the numerous types
of the law, we find the Redeemer abundantly foreshadowed.
Prophets and kings, priests and preachers, all look one way—
they all stand as the cherubs did over the ark, desiring to look
within, and to read the mystery of God's great propitiation.

Charles H. Spurgeon

ISAIAH 7:14

Therefore, the Lord himself will give you a sign: See, the virgin will conceive, have a son, and name him Immanuel.

PSALM 130

AWAITING REDEMPTION

A song of ascents.

¹ Out of the depths I call to you, LORD!
² Lord, listen to my voice;
let your ears be attentive
to my cry for help.

³ LORD, if you kept an account of iniquities,
Lord, who could stand?
⁴ But with you there is forgiveness,
so that you may be revered.

⁵ I wait for the LORD; I wait
and put my hope in his word.
⁶ I wait for the Lord
more than watchmen for the morning—
more than watchmen for the morning.

⁷ Israel, put your hope in the LORD.
For there is faithful love with the LORD,
and with him is redemption in abundance.
⁸ And he will redeem Israel
from all its iniquities.

CRAFT

DIFFICULTY ● ● ●

CRAFT TIME
20–25 hours

Share your progress by using #SheReadsTruth
or tagging @shereadstruth on social media.

"A Thrill of Hope"
Cross-Stitch

SUPPLIES

Size 14 navy cross-stitch fabric

Embroidery hoop (8-inch works well for this project)

Scissors

DMC embroidery floss in metallic gold and white (or, choose your own colors!)

Size 24 tapestry needle

Cross-stitch pattern

Scan this QR code to download this **cross-stitch pattern**!

TO BEGIN

Find the center of the pattern (marked) and the center of your fabric. This is where you'll begin stitching. Center fabric in the embroidery hoop and secure.

Cut a piece of white embroidery floss the length of your arm, separate out 2 of the 6 threads, then thread them through your needle. Set the remaining 4 threads aside to use as you need them, 2 at a time. *Note: If you use the gold thread, you will need to use 4 threads instead of 2.*

To begin stitching, bring the threaded needle up from the back of the fabric, leaving a tail of about an inch of floss behind the fabric. Stitch the next 3 or 4 stitches over the tail. Clip off the extra thread.

STITCHING

There are two methods. The first method is to work a row of half stitches ////, then work back \\\\ to complete the X's (see illustration). Use this method for most stitching. The second method is to complete each X as you go. Use this method for vertical or complex rows of stitches.

The sign of a real cross-stitch pro is when all of the X's are crossed in the same direction (that is, the top thread of the X always slants in the same direction, either \ or /). If you're a beginner, don't worry about this little detail. But if you're up for the challenge, give it a try!

FINISHING

When you come to the end of a thread, or to change to a new color, use your needle to weave the thread through the last 5 or 6 stitches on the back side of your fabric. Clip the thread short so as not to leave a loose tail. Then start your next color or another thread of the same color with the next stitch, securing the tail as you did before.

When your project is complete, remove it from the hoop. Before you display your work, smooth it and remove wrinkles by placing another cloth on top of the needlework and pressing lightly with a warm iron.

Display your finished creation in a frame or in an embroidery hoop.

Seek the Lord

Seek the LORD while he may be found; call to him while he is near.

ISAIAH 55:6

ISAIAH 55:6–13

⁶ Seek the LORD while he may be found;
   call to him while he is near.
⁷ Let the wicked one abandon his way
   and the sinful one his thoughts;
      let him return to the LORD,
         so he may have compassion on him,
            and to our God, for he will freely forgive.

⁸ "For my thoughts are not your thoughts,
   and your ways are not my ways."
This is the LORD's declaration.
⁹ "For as heaven is higher than earth,
so my ways are higher than your ways,
and my thoughts than your thoughts.
¹⁰ For just as rain and snow fall from heaven
and do not return there
without saturating the earth
and making it germinate and sprout,
and providing seed to sow
and food to eat,
¹¹ so my word that comes from my mouth
will not return to me empty,
but it will accomplish what I please
and will prosper in what I send it to do."

² You will indeed go out with joy
and be peacefully guided;
the mountains and the hills will break into singing before you,
and all the trees of the field will clap their hands.
³ Instead of the thornbush, a cypress will come up,
and instead of the brier, a myrtle will come up;
this will stand as a monument for the LORD,
an everlasting sign that will not be destroyed.

JOHN 7:37-38

⁷ On the last and most important day of the festival, Jesus stood up and cried out, "If anyone is thirsty, let him come to me and drink. ³⁸ The one who believes in me, as the Scripture has said, will have streams of living water flow from deep within him."

MATTHEW 11:28-30

²⁸ "Come to me, all of you who are weary and burdened, and I will give you rest. ²⁹ Take up my yoke and learn from me, because I am lowly and humble in heart, and you will find rest for your souls. ³⁰ For my yoke is easy and my burden is light."

REVELATION 3:20

²⁰ See! I stand at the door and knock. If anyone hears my voice and opens the door, I will come in to him and eat with him, and he with me."

ISAIAH 12:1-6

A SONG OF PRAISE

¹ On that day you will say:
"I will give thanks to you, LORD,
although you were angry with me.
Your anger has turned away,
and you have comforted me.
² Indeed, God is my salvation;
I will trust him and not be afraid,
for the LORD, the LORD himself,
is my strength and my song.
He has become my salvation."
³ You will joyfully draw water
from the springs of salvation,
⁴ and on that day you will say:
"Give thanks to the LORD; proclaim his name!
Make his works known among the peoples.
Declare that his name is exalted.
⁵ Sing to the LORD, for he has done glorious things.
Let this be known throughout the earth.
⁶ Cry out and sing, citizen of Zion,
for the Holy One of Israel is among you
in his greatness."

NOTES

LONG LAY
the
WORLD
IN SIN AND ERROR
PINING,
Till
HE APPEARED
and the
SOUL FELT
its
WORTH.

The First Promise of the Messiah

"He will strike your head, and you will strike his heel." GENESIS 3:15

GENESIS 3:1–15

THE TEMPTATION AND THE FALL

¹ Now the serpent was the most cunning of all the wild animals that the LORD God had made. He said to the woman, "Did God really say, 'You can't eat from any tree in the garden'?"

² The woman said to the serpent, "We may eat the fruit from the trees in the garden. ³ But about the fruit of the tree in the middle of the garden, God said, 'You must not eat it or touch it, or you will die.'"

⁴ "No! You will not die," the serpent said to the woman. ⁵ "In fact, God knows that when you eat it your eyes will be opened and you will be like God, knowing good and evil." ⁶ The woman saw that the tree was good for food and delightful to look at, and that it was desirable for obtaining wisdom. So she took some of its fruit and ate it; she also gave some to her husband, who was with her, and he ate it. ⁷ Then the eyes of both of them were opened, and they knew they were naked; so they sewed fig leaves together and made coverings for themselves.

SIN'S CONSEQUENCES

⁸ Then the man and his wife heard the sound of the LORD God walking in the garden at the time of the evening breeze, and they hid from the LORD God among the trees of the garden. ⁹ So the LORD God called out to the man and said to him, "Where are you?"

¹⁰ And he said, "I heard you in the garden, and I was afraid because I was naked, so I hid."

¹¹ Then he asked, "Who told you that you were naked? Did you eat from the tree that I commanded you not to eat from?"

¹² The man replied, "The woman you gave to be with me—she gave me some fruit from the tree, and I ate."

¹³ So the LORD God asked the woman, "What is this you have done?"

And the woman said, "The serpent deceived me, and I ate."

¹⁴ So the LORD God said to the serpent:

> Because you have done this,
> you are cursed more than any livestock
> and more than any wild animal.
> You will move on your belly
> and eat dust all the days of your life.
> ¹⁵ I will put hostility between you and the woman,
> and between your offspring and her offspring.
> He will strike your head,
> and you will strike his heel.

1 CORINTHIANS 15:45-49

⁴⁵ So it is written, The first man Adam became a living being; the last Adam became a life-giving spirit. ⁴⁶ However, the spiritual is not first, but the natural, then the spiritual.

⁴⁷ The first man was from the earth, a man of dust; the second man is from heaven. ⁴⁸ Like the man of dust, so are those who are of the dust; like the man of heaven, so are those who are of heaven. ⁴⁹ And just as we have borne the image of the man of dust, we will also bear the image of the man of heaven.

HEBREWS 2:14-16

¹⁴ Now since the children have flesh and blood in common, Jesus also shared in these, so that through his death he might destroy the one holding the power of death—that is, the devil— ¹⁵ and free those who were held in slavery all their lives by the fear of death. ¹⁶ For it is clear that he does not reach out to help angels, but to help Abraham's offspring.

Notes

DAY

1	2	**3**	4	5	6	7
8	9	10	11	12	13	14
15	16	17	18	19	20	21
22	23	24	25	26	27	28
29	30	31				

PREP TIME
5 minutes

COOK TIME
30 minutes

SERVINGS
5

INGREDIENTS

4 cups apple cider

½-inch nub of fresh ginger, minced

1 lemon, sliced

2 cinnamon sticks (additional for garnish, if desired)

⅛ teaspoon ground nutmeg

1½ teaspoons vanilla extract

3 star anise (optional)

5 whole allspice berries (optional)

DIRECTIONS

Combine ingredients in a large stock pot over medium low heat. Let simmer 30–45 minutes. Ladle into mugs, and garnish with a cinnamon stick.

Winter Wassail

DIFFICULTY

A Note from Raechel

I've tasted and tweaked a lot of wassail and cider recipes in the autumns and winters of my life, and this is hands-down my favorite. (Maybe it's the kick of lemon in place of oranges or apples?) This cozy drink has just the right balance of sweet and spice, with a velvety smooth finish. It will be ready to drink in just half an hour, but I recommend doubling the recipe and letting it simmer on your stovetop all day long. Your whole house will smell like Christmas, and I cannot imagine it going to waste.

God's Covenant with Abram

"All the peoples on earth will be blessed through you." GENESIS 12:3

GENESIS 12:1–9

THE CALL OF ABRAM

¹ The LORD said to Abram:

Go out from your land,
your relatives,
and your father's house
to the land that I will show you.
² I will make you into a great nation,
I will bless you,
I will make your name great,
and you will be a blessing.
³ I will bless those who bless you,
I will curse anyone who treats you with contempt,
and all the peoples on earth
will be blessed through you.

⁴ So Abram went, as the LORD had told him, and Lot went with him. Abram was seventy-five years old when he left Haran. ⁵ He took his wife Sarai, his nephew Lot, all the possessions they had accumulated, and the people they had acquired in Haran, and they set out for the land of Canaan. When they came to the land of Canaan, ⁶ Abram passed through the land to the site of Shechem, at the oak of Moreh. (At that time the Canaanites were in the land.) ⁷ The LORD appeared to Abram and said, "To your offspring I will give this land." So he built an altar

there to the LORD who had appeared to him. ⁸ From there he moved on to the hill country east of Bethel and pitched his tent, with Bethel on the west and Ai on the east. He built an altar to the LORD there, and he called on the name of the LORD. ⁹ Then Abram journeyed by stages to the Negev.

GENESIS 21:1-7

THE BIRTH OF ISAAC

¹ The LORD came to Sarah as he had said, and the LORD did for Sarah what he had promised. ² Sarah became pregnant and bore a son to Abraham in his old age, at the appointed time God had told him. ³ Abraham named his son who was born to him—the one Sarah bore to him—Isaac. ⁴ When his son Isaac was eight days old, Abraham circumcised him, as God had commanded him. ⁵ Abraham was a hundred years old when his son Isaac was born to him.

⁶ Sarah said, "God has made me laugh, and everyone who hears will laugh with me." ⁷ She also said, "Who would have told Abraham that Sarah would nurse children? Yet I have borne a son for him in his old age."

GENESIS 22:15-18

¹⁵ Then the angel of the LORD called to Abraham a second time from heaven ¹⁶ and said, "By myself I have sworn," this is the LORD's declaration: "Because you have done this thing and have not withheld your only son,

¹⁷ I will indeed bless you and make your offspring as numerous as the stars of the sky and the sand on the seashore.

Your offspring will possess the city gates of their enemies. ¹⁸ And all the nations of the earth will be blessed by your offspring because you have obeyed my command."

JOHN 8:54-58

⁵⁴ "If I glorify myself," Jesus answered, "my glory is nothing. My Father—about whom you say, 'He is our God'—he is the one who glorifies me. ⁵⁵ You do not know him, but I know him. If I were to say I don't know him, I would be a liar like you. But I do know him, and I keep his word. ⁵⁶ Your father Abraham rejoiced to see my day; he saw it and was glad."

⁵⁷ The Jews replied, "You aren't fifty years old yet, and you've seen Abraham?"

⁵⁸ Jesus said to them, "Truly I tell you, before Abraham was, I am."

Notes

DAY

1	2	3	4	5	6	7
8	9	10	11	12	13	14
15	16	17	18	19	20	21
22	23	24	25	26	27	28
29	30	31				

The Root and Descendant of David

Then a shoot will grow from the stump of Jesse, and a branch from his roots will bear fruit. ISAIAH 11:1

2 SAMUEL 7:8–16

[8] "So now this is what you are to say to my servant David: 'This is what the LORD of Armies says: I took you from the pasture, from tending the flock, to be ruler over my people Israel. [9] I have been with you wherever you have gone, and I have destroyed all your enemies before you. I will make a great name for you like that of the greatest on the earth. [10] I will designate a place for my people Israel and plant them, so that they may live there and not be disturbed again. Evildoers will not continue to oppress them as they have done [11] ever since the day I ordered judges to be over my people Israel. I will give you rest from all your enemies.

"'The LORD declares to you: The LORD himself will make a house for you. [12] When your time comes and you rest with your fathers, I will raise up after you your descendant, who will come from your body, and I will establish his kingdom. [13] He is the one who will build a house for my name, and I will establish the throne of his kingdom forever. [14] I will be his father, and he will be my son. When he does wrong, I will discipline him with a rod of men and blows from mortals. [15] But my faithful love will never leave him as it did when I removed it from Saul, whom I removed from before you. [16] Your house and kingdom will endure before me forever, and your throne will be established forever.'"

JEREMIAH 23:1-8

THE LORD AND HIS SHEEP

[1] "Woe to the shepherds who destroy and scatter the sheep of my pasture!" This is the LORD's declaration. [2] "Therefore, this is what the LORD, the God of Israel, says about the shepherds who tend my people: You have scattered my flock, banished them, and have not attended to them. I am about to attend to you because of your evil acts"—this is the LORD's declaration. [3] "I will gather the remnant of my flock from all the lands where I have banished them, and I will return them to their grazing land. They will become fruitful and numerous. [4] I will raise up shepherds over them who will tend them. They will no longer be afraid or discouraged, nor will any be missing." This is the LORD's declaration.

THE RIGHTEOUS BRANCH OF DAVID

[5] "Look, the days are coming"—this is the LORD's declaration—
"when I will raise up a Righteous Branch for David.
He will reign wisely as king
and administer justice and righteousness in the land.

[6] In his days Judah will be saved,
and Israel will dwell securely.
This is the name he will be called:
The LORD Is Our Righteousness.

[7] "Look, the days are coming"—the LORD's declaration—"when it will no longer be said, 'As the LORD lives who brought the Israelites from the land of Egypt,' [8] but, 'As the LORD lives, who brought and led the descendants of the house of Israel from the land of the north and from all the other countries where I had banished them.' They will dwell once more in their own land."

ISAIAH 11:1-6

REIGN OF THE DAVIDIC KING

[1] Then a shoot will grow from the stump of Jesse,
and a branch from his roots will bear fruit.
[2] The Spirit of the LORD will rest on him—
a Spirit of wisdom and understanding,
a Spirit of counsel and strength,
a Spirit of knowledge and of the fear of the LORD.
[3] His delight will be in the fear of the LORD.
He will not judge
by what he sees with his eyes,
he will not execute justice
by what he hears with his ears,

HOW COULD JESUS RECEIVE DAVID'S THRONE? DIDN'T GOD END THAT ROYAL LINE?

The prophet Jeremiah records these words from God about wicked King Coniah (also known as Jeconiah and Jehoiachin): "None of his descendants will succeed in sitting on the throne of David" (Jr 22:30). But Matthew includes Jeconiah in Jesus's lineage (Mt 1:11–12). In His sovereignty, God made a way for Jesus to come from David's "body" (2Sm 7:12) without also being a descendant of Jeconiah. While Matthew provides Jesus's ancestry through His adoptive father, Joseph, and therefore His legal right to Solomon's throne, Luke gives us Jesus's bloodline through His mother, Mary, who is descended from David's son Nathan (Lk 3:31), but not from Jeconiah. In other words, God's promises cannot be thwarted.

[4] but he will judge the poor righteously
and execute justice for the oppressed of the land.
He will strike the land
with a scepter from his mouth,
and he will kill the wicked
with a command from his lips.
[5] Righteousness will be a belt around his hips;
faithfulness will be a belt around his waist.

[6] The wolf will dwell with the lamb,
and the leopard will lie down with the goat.
The calf, the young lion, and the fattened calf will be together,
and a child will lead them.

MATTHEW 12:22–23

[22] Then a demon-possessed man who was blind and unable to speak was brought to him. He healed him, so that the man could both speak and see. [23] All the crowds were astounded and said, "Could this be the Son of David?"

MATTHEW 22:41–46

THE QUESTION ABOUT THE CHRIST

[41] While the Pharisees were together, Jesus questioned them, [42] "What do you think about the Messiah? Whose son is he?"

They replied, "David's."

[43] He asked them, "How is it then that David, inspired by the Spirit, calls him 'Lord'

[44] The Lord declared to my Lord,
'Sit at my right hand
until I put your enemies under your feet'?

[45] "If David calls him 'Lord,' how then can he be his son?" [46] No one was able to answer him at all, and from that day no one dared to question him anymore.

REVELATION 22:16

"I, Jesus, have sent my angel to attest these things to you for the churches. I am the Root and descendant of David, the bright morning star."

Notes

DAY

1	2	3	4	**5**	6	7
8	9	10	11	12	13	14
15	16	17	18	19	20	21
22	23	24	25	26	27	28
29	30	31				

HYMN

O Holy Night

TEXT

Placide Cappeau, 1847

TUNE

Cantique de Noel

TRANSLATED

John S. Dwight

A thrill of hope, the weary world rejoices.

O holy night! the stars are brightly shining;
It is the night of the dear Savior's birth.
Long lay the world in sin and error pining,
Till He appeared and the soul felt its worth.
A thrill of hope, the weary world rejoices,
For yonder breaks a new and glorious morn.
Fall on your knees, O hear the angel voices!
O night divine, O night when Christ was born!
O night divine, O night, O night divine!

Truly He taught us to love one another;
His law is love and His gospel is peace.
Chains shall He break for the slave is our
    brother,
And in His name all oppression shall cease.
Sweet hymns of joy in grateful chorus raise we;
Let all within us praise His holy name!
Christ is the Lord! O praise His name forever!
His pow'r and glory evermore proclaim!
His pow'r and glory evermore proclaim!

1. O ho-ly night, the stars are bright-ly shin-ing; It is the night of the dear Sav-ior's birth!

3. Tru-ly He taught us to love one a-noth-er; His law is love and His gos-pel is peace.

Long lay the world in sin and er-ror pin-ing, Till He ap-peared and the soul felt its worth.

Chains shall He break for the slave is our broth-er, And in His name all op-press-ion shall cease.

A thrill of hope, the wea-ry world re-joic-es, For yon-der breaks a new and glo-rious morn.

Sweet hymns of joy in grate-ful cho-rus raise we, Let all with-in us praise His ho-ly name!

Fall on your knees, O hear the an-gel voic-es! O night di-vine,

Christ is the Lord! O praise His name for-ev-er! His pow'r and glo-

O night when Christ was born! O night di-vine, O night, O night di-vine!

ry ev-er-more pro-claim! His pow'r and glo-ry ev-er-more pro-claim!

A Redeemer from Bethlehem

One will come from you to be ruler over Israel for me. MICAH 5:2

MICAH 5:2-5a

2 Bethlehem Ephrathah,
you are small among the clans of Judah;
one will come from you
to be ruler over Israel for me.
His origin is from antiquity,
from ancient times.
3 Therefore, Israel will be abandoned until the time
when she who is in labor has given birth;
then the rest of the ruler's brothers will return
to the people of Israel.
4 He will stand and shepherd them
in the strength of the Lord,
in the majestic name of the Lord his God.
They will live securely,
for then his greatness will extend
to the ends of the earth.
5 He will be their peace.

NUMBERS 24:17a

I see him, but not now;
I perceive him, but not near.
A star will come from Jacob,
and a scepter will arise from Israel.

RUTH 4:11-17

[11] All the people who were at the city gate, including the elders, said, "We are witnesses. May the LORD make the woman who is entering your house like Rachel and Leah, who together built the house of Israel.

> May you be powerful in Ephrathah and your name well known in Bethlehem.

[12] May your house become like the house of Perez, the son Tamar bore to Judah, because of the offspring the LORD will give you by this young woman."

[13] Boaz took Ruth and she became his wife. He slept with her, and the LORD granted conception to her, and she gave birth to a son. [14] The women said to Naomi, "Blessed be the LORD, who has not left you without a family redeemer today. May his name become well known in Israel. [15] He will renew your life and sustain you in your old age. Indeed, your daughter-in-law, who loves you and is better to you than seven sons, has given birth to him." [16] Naomi took the child, placed him on her lap, and became his nanny. [17] The neighbor women said, "A son has been born to Naomi," and they named him Obed. He was the father of Jesse, the father of David.

LUKE 2:4

Joseph also went up from the town of Nazareth in Galilee, to Judea, to the city of David, which is called Bethlehem, because he was of the house and family line of David…

JOHN 7:40-44

THE PEOPLE ARE DIVIDED OVER JESUS

[40] When some from the crowd heard these words, they said, "This truly is the Prophet." [41] Others said, "This is the Messiah." But some said, "Surely the Messiah doesn't come from Galilee, does he? [42] Doesn't the Scripture say that the Messiah comes from David's offspring and from the town of Bethlehem, where David lived?" [43] So the crowd was divided because of him. [44] Some of them wanted to seize him, but no one laid hands on him.

Notes

DAY

1	2	3	4	5	6	7
8	9	10	11	12	13	14
15	16	17	18	19	20	21
22	23	24	25	26	27	28
29	30	31				

Candied Pecans

DIFFICULTY ● ○ ○

A Note from Raechel

Candied pecans remind me of the "Dickens of a Christmas" festival our small town holds on Main Street every December. Even in the open air, you can smell the sweet, spicy nuts from a block away. I always assumed we were at the mercy of the man wearing the period top hat and fingerless gloves to provide us with this traditional treat every year, until I discovered how simple it is to make them at home. Send these to school as part of a teacher's gift, delight your host with a still-warm treat, or start them in your oven at home and watch friends and family come out of the woodwork to taste what you're cooking.

For a sweet and spicy treat, add a bit of cayenne pepper to the dry mixture, to taste.

PREP TIME
5 minutes

COOK TIME
1 hour

SERVINGS
16

INGREDIENTS

1 egg white

1 tablespoon water

1 pound (4 cups) shelled pecan halves

1 cup sugar

2 teaspoons cinnamon

1 teaspoon salt

DIRECTIONS

Preheat oven to 250°F and prepare a large baking sheet with a silicone mat or cooking spray.

Beat egg white and water with a whisk in a large bowl. Add pecans and toss until well coated.

In a smaller bowl, combine sugar, cinnamon, and salt. Add to pecans and turn over until well coated.

Arrange pecans in a single layer on prepared baking sheet and bake 1 hour, stirring every 15 minutes.

Allow to cool (try not to burn your mouth tasting them!) and store in an airtight container up to one week or in the freezer up to six months.

GRACE DAY

7

Advent is a season of anticipation and celebration. The weary world
rejoices at the Messiah's first advent, even as we long for His return. Use
this day to pray, rest, and reflect on the hope we have because Christ left
the glories of heaven to be born in Bethlehem.

God's love was revealed among us in this way: God sent his one and only Son into the world so that we might live through him.

1 JOHN 4:9

Copper Evergreen Wreath

DIFFICULTY ● ● ○

CRAFT TIME
1 hour

MATERIALS

Assorted greens (fir, cedar, pine, spruce, boxwood, eucalyptus, etc.)

Copper hoop (available at craft stores or online)

Green or black zip ties

22 gauge floral wire

Wire cutters

Fresh trimmings (pine cones, cotton, dried flowers, berries)

Ribbon

Spray bottle

DIRECTIONS

This wreath is built one cluster of greenery at a time. Begin by tying a small cluster of greenery onto your hoop with a zip tie. Secure tie with a few wraps of floral tape so it doesn't slide.

Continue layering clusters, one after another in the same direction, making sure to cover zip ties with the next set of greens. Stop at bottom of hoop.

Repeat on the other side of hoop, working from mid-height to bottom center.

Fill in bottom center area with more greenery to cover last clusters and zip ties. Secure with wire.

Next, tie on ribbon (if desired) and secure fresh trimmings with wire.

Spritz wreath generously with water every other day to keep it looking fresh and green throughout the holiday season. Spraying from the back helps keep water off the trimmings.

. . .

The Second Sunday of Advent

DAY 8

Angels Sunday

It is the wonder of angels that the love of Jesus should be set upon poor, lost, guilty humanity. Each believer must, when filled with a sense of Jesus's love, also be overwhelmed with astonishment that such love should be lavished on an object so utterly unworthy of it.

Charles H. Spurgeon

LUKE 2:13–14

Suddenly there was a multitude of the
heavenly host with the angel, praising
God and saying:

Glory to God in the highest heaven,
and peace on earth to people he favors!

HYMN

O Come, All Ye Faithful

TEXT AND TUNE

John F. Wade, ca 1743

TRANSLATION

Frederick Oakley, 1841

O come, all ye faithful, joyful and triumphant,
O come ye, O come ye to Bethlehem;
Come and behold Him, born the King of
    angels;
O come, let us adore Him,
O come, let us adore Him,
O come, let us adore Him, Christ the Lord.

Sing, choirs of angels, sing in exultation,
sing, all ye citizens of heaven above;
glory to God, all glory in the highest;
O come, let us adore Him,
O come, let us adore Him,
O come, let us adore Him, Christ the Lord.

Yea, Lord, we greet Thee, born this happy
    morning,
Jesus, to Thee be all glory given;
Word of the Father, now in flesh appearing;
O come, let us adore Him,
O come, let us adore Him,
O come, let us adore Him, Christ the Lord.

*Glory to God, all glory
in the highest.*

1 O come, all ye faith - ful, joy - ful and tri - um - phant, O
2 Sing, choirs of an - gels, sing in ex - ul - ta - tion,
3 Yea, Lord, we greet Thee, born this hap - py mor - ning,

come ye, O come____ ye to Beth - - le - hem;
sing, all ye ci - ti - zens of heaven____ a - bove;
Je - sus, to Thee____ be all glo - - ry given;

Come and be - hold Him, born the King of an - gels;
glo - ry to God, all glo - ry in the high - est;
Word of the Fa - ther, now in flesh ap - pear - ing;

Refrain

O come, let us a - dore Him, O come, let us a - dore Him,

O come, let us a - dore Him,____ Christ,____ the Lord.

God with Us

The Son is the radiance of God's glory and the exact expression of his nature... HEBREWS 1:3

ISAIAH 7:14

Therefore, the Lord himself will give you a sign: See, the virgin will conceive, have a son, and name him Immanuel.

HEBREWS 1:1–3

THE NATURE OF THE SON

¹ Long ago God spoke to the fathers by the prophets at different times and in different ways. ² In these last days, he has spoken to us by his Son. God has appointed him heir of all things and made the universe through him. ³ The Son is the radiance of God's glory and the exact expression of his nature, sustaining all things by his powerful word. After making purification for sins, he sat down at the right hand of the Majesty on high.

MATTHEW 1:22–23

²² Now all this took place to fulfill what was spoken by the Lord through the prophet:

²³ See, the virgin will become pregnant
and give birth to a son,
and they will name him Immanuel,

which is translated "God is with us."

ARE *IMMANUEL* AND *JESUS* THE SAME NAME?

Jesus is a proper name, while *Immanuel* is a prophetic promise that God would be with His people. Immanuel, or "God is with us," was a description of what the coming Messiah would be like— someone who understands the needs, struggles, and hopes of humanity. The angel tells Joseph to name the child Jesus because "he will save his people from their sins" (Mt 1:23). When Matthew connects the prophecy from Isaiah 7:14 to Jesus, he is saying that this child is the fulfillment of that promise of long ago.

JOHN 10:31-39

31 Again the Jews picked up rocks to stone him.

32 Jesus replied, "I have shown you many good works from the Father. For which of these works are you stoning me?"

33 "We aren't stoning you for a good work," the Jews answered, "but for blasphemy, because you—being a man—make yourself God."

34 Jesus answered them, "Isn't it written in your law, I said, you are gods? 35 If he called those whom the word of God came to 'gods'—and the Scripture cannot be broken— 36 do you say, 'You are blaspheming' to the one the Father set apart and sent into the world, because I said: I am the Son of God? 37 If I am not doing my Father's works, don't believe me. 38 But if I am doing them and you don't believe me, believe the works. This way you will know and understand that the Father is in me and I in the Father." 39 Then they were trying again to seize him, but he eluded their grasp.

JOHN 14:6-11

6 Jesus told him, "I am the way, the truth, and the life. No one comes to the Father except through me.

7 If you know me, you will also know my Father. From now on you do know him and have seen him."

8 "Lord," said Philip, "show us the Father, and that's enough for us."

9 Jesus said to him, "Have I been among you all this time and you do not know me, Philip? The one who has seen me has seen the Father. How can you say, 'Show us the Father'? 10 Don't you believe that I am in the Father and the Father is in me? The words I speak to you I do not speak on my own. The Father who lives in me does his works. 11 Believe me that I am in the Father and the Father is in me. Otherwise, believe because of the works themselves.

1 JOHN 4:9-10

9 God's love was revealed among us in this way: God sent his one and only Son into the world so that we might live through him. 10 Love consists in this: not that we loved God, but that he loved us and sent his Son to be the atoning sacrifice for our sins.

Notes

DAY

1	2	3	4	5	6	7
8	**9**	10	11	12	13	14
15	16	17	18	19	20	21
22	23	24	25	26	27	28
29	30	31				

Bethlehem in Scripture

Bethlehem is best known as the birthplace of Jesus, but the town's significance is foreshadowed throughout the Old Testament. Here are the key places where Bethlehem appears in Scripture.

GENESIS 35:19	JUDGES 17:7–13	JUDGES 19:1	RUTH 1:1–2, 19, 22; 2:4; 4:11	1 SAMUEL 16:1–13	2 SAMUEL 2:32
Jacob's wife Rachel died and was buried on their way to Bethlehem.	Bethlehem was the hometown of the Levite who became Micah's priest.	The concubine of the Levite in Judges 19 was from Bethlehem.	Naomi, Ruth's mother-in-law, was from Bethlehem. Ruth met and married Boaz in Bethlehem, and the elders blessed them, that their name would be "well known in Bethlehem."	David, Ruth's great grandson, grew up in Bethlehem. Samuel came to Bethlehem to anoint young David as Israel's future king.	King David's soldier Asahel was killed by the commander of Saul's army, Abner, and was buried in his father Zeruiah's tomb in Bethlehem.

2 SAMUEL 23:14	2 CHRONICLES 11:5–6	JEREMIAH 41:17 EZRA 2:21	MICAH 5:2	MATTHEW 2:1–12 LUKE 2:4–20 JOHN 7:42
The Philistines occupied Bethlehem when David's mighty men snuck behind enemy lines to bring David a drink of water from the well by the town gate.	Bethlehem was one of King Rehoboam's fortified cities, built to protect Judah after the kingdom of Israel divided.	Bethlehem is mentioned as one of the cities directly affected by the Babylonian exile.	The prophet Micah foretold that the Messiah, the ancient One, would come from Bethlehem.	Jesus Christ was born in Bethlehem.

A THRILL *of* HOPE—
the WEARY WORLD
REJOICES, *for*
YONDER BREAKS
A NEW *and*
GLORIOUS MORN!

The Law of God Fulfilled

"Don't think that I came to abolish the Law or the Prophets. I did not come to abolish but to fulfill." MATTHEW 5:17

EXODUS 20:1–17

THE TEN COMMANDMENTS

¹ Then God spoke all these words:

² I am the LORD your God, who brought you out of the land of Egypt, out of the place of slavery.

³ Do not have other gods besides me.

⁴ Do not make an idol for yourself, whether in the shape of anything in the heavens above or on the earth below or in the waters under the earth. ⁵ Do not bow in worship to them, and do not serve them; for I, the LORD your God, am a jealous God, punishing the children for the fathers' iniquity, to the third and fourth generations of those who hate me, ⁶ but showing faithful love to a thousand generations of those who love me and keep my commands.

⁷ Do not misuse the name of the LORD your God, because the LORD will not leave anyone unpunished who misuses his name.

⁸ Remember the Sabbath day, to keep it holy: ⁹ You are to labor six days and do all your work, ¹⁰ but the seventh day is a Sabbath to the LORD your God. You must not do any work—you, your son or daughter, your male or female servant, your livestock, or the resident alien who is within your city gates. ¹¹ For the LORD made the heavens and the earth, the sea, and everything in them in six

days; then he rested on the seventh day. Therefore the LORD blessed the Sabbath day and declared it holy.

[12] Honor your father and your mother so that you may have a long life in the land that the LORD your God is giving you.

[13] Do not murder.

[14] Do not commit adultery.

[15] Do not steal.

[16] Do not give false testimony against your neighbor.

[17] Do not covet your neighbor's house. Do not covet your neighbor's wife, his male or female servant, his ox or donkey, or anything that belongs to your neighbor.

MATTHEW 5:17-19

CHRIST FULFILLS THE LAW

[17] "Don't think that I came to abolish the Law or the Prophets. I did not come to abolish but to fulfill. [18] For truly I tell you, until heaven and earth pass away, not the smallest letter or one stroke of a letter will pass away from the law until all things are accomplished. [19] Therefore, whoever breaks one of the least of these commands and teaches others to do the same will be called least in the kingdom of heaven. But whoever does and teaches these commands will be called great in the kingdom of heaven."

ROMANS 8:1-4

THE LIFE-GIVING SPIRIT

[1] Therefore, there is now no condemnation for those in Christ Jesus, [2] because the law of the Spirit of life in Christ Jesus has set you free from the law of sin and death.

[3] What the law could not do since it was weakened by the flesh, God did.

He condemned sin in the flesh by sending his own Son in the likeness of sinful flesh as a sin offering, [4] in order that the law's requirement would be fulfilled in us who do not walk according to the flesh but according to the Spirit.

Notes

DAY						
1	2	3	4	5	6	7
8	9	**10**	11	12	13	14
15	16	17	18	19	20	21
22	23	24	25	26	27	28
29	30	31				

Righteousness Through Christ

The righteousness of God is through faith in Jesus Christ to all who believe… ROMANS 3:22

JOHN 1:1–5, 14–18

PROLOGUE

[1] In the beginning was the Word, and the Word was with God, and the Word was God. [2] He was with God in the beginning. [3] All things were created through him, and apart from him not one thing was created that has been created. [4] In him was life, and that life was the light of men. [5] That light shines in the darkness, and yet the darkness did not overcome it.

…

[14] The Word became flesh and dwelt among us.

We observed his glory, the glory as the one and only Son from the Father, full of grace and truth. [15] (John testified concerning him and exclaimed, "This was the one of whom I said, 'The one coming after me ranks ahead of me, because he existed before me.'") [16] Indeed, we have all received grace upon grace from his fullness, [17] for the law was given through Moses; grace and truth came through Jesus Christ. [18] No one has ever seen God. The one and only Son, who is himself God and is at the Father's side—he has revealed him.

ROMANS 3:21-28

THE RIGHTEOUSNESS OF GOD THROUGH FAITH

[21] But now, apart from the law, the righteousness of God has been revealed, attested by the Law and the Prophets. [22] The righteousness of God is through faith in Jesus Christ to all who believe, since there is no distinction. [23] For all have sinned and fall short of the glory of God. [24] They are justified freely by his grace through the redemption that is in Christ Jesus. [25] God presented him as an atoning sacrifice in his blood, received through faith, to demonstrate his righteousness, because in his restraint God passed over the sins previously committed. [26] God presented him to demonstrate his righteousness at the present time, so that he would be righteous and declare righteous the one who has faith in Jesus.

BOASTING EXCLUDED

[27] Where, then, is boasting? It is excluded. By what kind of law? By one of works? No, on the contrary, by a law of faith. [28] For we conclude that a person is justified by faith apart from the works of the law.

EPHESIANS 1:7-10

[7] In him we have redemption through his blood, the forgiveness of our trespasses, according to the riches of his grace [8] that he richly poured out on us with all wisdom and understanding. [9] He made known to us the mystery of his will, according to his good pleasure that he purposed in Christ [10] as a plan for the right time—to bring everything together in Christ, both things in heaven and things on earth in him.

COLOSSIANS 1:13-14

[13] He has rescued us from the domain of darkness and transferred us into the kingdom of the Son he loves.

[14] In him we have redemption, the forgiveness of sins.

An All-Sufficient Sacrifice

"Though your sins are scarlet, they will be as white as snow."
ISAIAH 1:18

ISAIAH 1:11, 18

[11] "What are all your sacrifices to me?"
asks the LORD.
"I have had enough of burnt offerings and rams
and the fat of well-fed cattle;
I have no desire for the blood of bulls,
lambs, or male goats.

…

[18] "Come, let us settle this,"
says the LORD.
"Though your sins are scarlet,
they will be as white as snow;
though they are crimson red,
they will be like wool."

ISAIAH 53:2–12

[2] He grew up before him like a young plant
and like a root out of dry ground.
He didn't have an impressive form
or majesty that we should look at him,
no appearance that we should desire him.
[3] He was despised and rejected by men,
a man of suffering who knew what sickness was.
He was like someone people turned away from;
he was despised, and we didn't value him.

[4] Yet he himself bore our sicknesses,
and he carried our pains;
but we in turn regarded him stricken,
struck down by God, and afflicted.
[5] But he was pierced because of our rebellion,
crushed because of our iniquities;
punishment for our peace was on him,
and we are healed by his wounds.
[6] We all went astray like sheep;
we all have turned to our own way;
and the LORD has punished him
for the iniquity of us all.

[7] He was oppressed and afflicted,
yet he did not open his mouth.
Like a lamb led to the slaughter
and like a sheep silent before her shearers,
he did not open his mouth.
[8] He was taken away because of oppression
and judgment;
and who considered his fate?

For he was cut off from the land of the living;
he was struck because of my people's rebellion.
⁹ He was assigned a grave with the wicked,
but he was with a rich man at his death,
because he had done no violence
and had not spoken deceitfully.

¹⁰ Yet the LORD was pleased to crush him severely.
When you make him a guilt offering,
he will see his seed, he will prolong his days,
and by his hand, the LORD's pleasure will be accomplished.
¹¹ After his anguish,
he will see light and be satisfied.
By his knowledge,
my righteous servant will justify many,
and he will carry their iniquities.
¹² Therefore I will give him the many as a portion,
and he will receive the mighty as spoil,
because he willingly submitted to death,
and was counted among the rebels;
yet he bore the sin of many
and interceded for the rebels.

JOHN 1:29

The next day John saw Jesus coming toward him and said,

"Here is the Lamb of God, who takes away the sin of the world!"

HEBREWS 9:11-14

NEW COVENANT MINISTRY

¹¹ But Christ has appeared as a high priest of the good things that have come. In the greater and more perfect tabernacle not made with hands (that is, not of this creation), ¹² he entered the most holy place once for all time, not by the blood of goats and calves, but by his own blood, having obtained eternal redemption. ¹³ For if the blood of goats and bulls and the ashes of a young cow, sprinkling those who are defiled, sanctify for the purification of the flesh, ¹⁴ how much more will the blood of Christ, who through the eternal Spirit offered himself without blemish to God, cleanse our consciences from dead works so that we can serve the living God?

HEBREWS 10:1-14

THE PERFECT SACRIFICE

¹ Since the law has only a shadow of the good things to come, and not the reality itself of those things, it can never perfect the worshipers by the same sacrifices they continually offer year after year. ² Otherwise, wouldn't they have stopped being offered, since the worshipers, purified once and for all, would no longer have any consciousness of sins? ³ But in the sacrifices there is a reminder of sins year after year. ⁴ For it is impossible for the blood of bulls and goats to take away sins.

⁵ Therefore, as he was coming into the world, he said:

You did not desire sacrifice and offering,
but you prepared a body for me.
⁶ You did not delight
in whole burnt offerings and sin offerings.
⁷ Then I said, "See—
it is written about me
in the scroll—
I have come to do your will, O God."

⁸ After he says above, You did not desire or delight in sacrifices and offerings, whole burnt offerings and sin offerings (which are offered according to the law), ⁹ he then says, See, I have come to do your will. He takes away the first to establish the second. ¹⁰ By this will, we have been sanctified through the offering of the body of Jesus Christ once for all time.

¹¹ Every priest stands day after day ministering and offering the same sacrifices time after time, which can never take away sins. ¹² But this man, after offering one sacrifice for sins forever, sat down at the right hand of God. ¹³ He is now waiting until his enemies are made his footstool. ¹⁴ For by one offering he has perfected forever those who are sanctified.

Notes

1	2	3	4	5	6	7
8	9	10	11	**12**	13	14
15	16	17	18	19	20	21
22	23	24	25	26	27	28
29	30	31				

A Gingerbread Cottage for the Shes

DIFFICULTY

PREP TIME
2 hours, plus overnight

COOK TIME
25 minutes

SERVINGS
1 gingerbread house

A Note from Raechel

I confess, I'd never made a gingerbread house from scratch before this one. We've always been content to come by our cookie cottages the old fashioned way: pick up a premade kit at the grocery store, plaster it with candy and frosting, and *Merry Christmas!* Another activity checked off the list. But this year, I wanted the experience of taking it slow—baking my own gingerbread and decorating something truly beautiful. This recipe isn't quick, and I wouldn't even say it's easy. But for you Shes who love to lean into a really special project: this is for you. I've tested it twice, and even made a printable template for you (complete with an SRT logo window!). I sure hope you love it as much as I do!

Gingerbread Dough

INGREDIENTS

1¼ cups packed dark brown sugar

¾ cup unsulfured molasses

½ cup (1 stick) unsalted butter

1 tablespoon ground cinnamon

1 tablespoon ground ginger

½ teaspoon coarse salt

1¼ cups milk

1 tablespoon baking powder

6½ cups all-purpose flour

DIRECTIONS

Combine brown sugar, molasses, butter, cinnamon, ginger, and salt in a medium saucepan over low heat, stirring until sugar is dissolved, about 10 minutes. Stir in milk, remove from heat, and let cool.

Pour cooled milk mixture into the bowl of a stand mixer fitted with the flat paddle attachment. Add baking powder and flour. Beginning on low speed and increasing to medium, mix until well combined.

Divide dough in half, shape into discs, and wrap in plastic to refrigerate overnight.

Royal Icing

INGREDIENTS

4 cups (about 1 pound) confectioners' sugar

3 tablespoons meringue powder

4–5 tablespoons water, plus more if needed

DIRECTIONS

Beat all ingredients together at low speed until icing forms peaks, about 7 to 10 minutes. Use immediately, or transfer to an airtight container.

Thin icing as needed by stirring in additional water, one teaspoon at a time.

Caramel Syrup

INGREDIENTS

1⅓ cups sugar

¾ cup water

DIRECTIONS

In a medium saucepan, bring sugar and water to a boil. Boil over medium-high heat until thickened and light brown, about 11 minutes. Use immediately.

ASSEMBLY INSTRUCTIONS

The day before you plan to construct your gingerbread house, prepare the gingerbread dough and refrigerate it overnight.

Once the dough has had plenty of time to chill, roll it out on a lightly-floured surface to about ⅛-inch thick. Chill again until firm, about 1 hour.

Preheat oven to 350°F. Once the rolled-out dough is firm, remove from fridge and cut out template shapes using a utility or paring knife (you can also use a pizza cutter and a straight edge). Transfer shapes to parchment-lined baking sheets and bake about 15 minutes, rotating sheets halfway through cooking time. Let cool completely.

While gingerbread cools, prepare royal icing, then caramel syrup.

Working quickly, assemble the gingerbread house using caramel syrup as the "glue." Start by dipping one edge of the front piece in caramel, then join coated edge to a side piece, forming a corner. Continue assembly by either dipping pieces in caramel syrup or brushing it on with a small paintbrush. Attach roof pieces last.

Place royal icing in a pastry bag fitted with a small, plain tip (or use a gallon plastic bag with a small snip off the corner). Have fun outlining the windows and doorway, decorating the roof, and making icicles. Finish it off with a snowstorm of confectioners' sugar!

Scan this QR code to download the **gingerbread house template**.

All Nations Shall Find Peace

They will beat their swords into plows and their spears into pruning knives. MICAH 4:3

MICAH 4:1–7

THE LORD'S RULE FROM RESTORED ZION

¹ In the last days
the mountain of the LORD's house
will be established
at the top of the mountains
 and will be raised above the hills.
  Peoples will stream to it,
  ² and many nations will come and say,
  "Come, let us go up to the mountain of the LORD,
 to the house of the God of Jacob.
He will teach us about his ways
so we may walk in his paths."
For instruction will go out of Zion
and the word of the LORD from Jerusalem.
³ He will settle disputes among many peoples
and provide arbitration for strong nations
that are far away.
They will beat their swords into plows
and their spears into pruning knives.
Nation will not take up the sword against nation,
and they will never again train for war.

⁴ But each person will sit under his grapevine
and under his fig tree
with no one to frighten him.
For the mouth of the LORD of Armies
has spoken.
⁵ Though all the peoples each walk
in the name of their gods,
we will walk in the name of the LORD our God
forever and ever.
⁶ On that day—
this is the LORD's declaration—
I will assemble the lame
and gather the scattered,
those I have injured.
⁷ I will make the lame into a remnant,
those far removed into a strong nation.
Then the LORD will reign over them in Mount Zion
from this time on and forever.

PSALM 46:4–11

⁴ There is a river—
its streams delight the city of God,
the holy dwelling place of the Most High.
⁵ God is within her; she will not be toppled.
God will help her when the morning dawns.
⁶ Nations rage, kingdoms topple;
the earth melts when he lifts his voice.

⁷ The LORD of Armies is with us;
the God of Jacob is our stronghold.   *Selah*

⁸ Come, see the works of the LORD,
who brings devastation on the earth.
⁹ He makes wars cease throughout the earth.
He shatters bows and cuts spears to pieces;
he sets wagons ablaze.
¹⁰ "Stop your fighting, and know that I am God,
exalted among the nations, exalted on the earth."
¹¹ The LORD of Armies is with us;
the God of Jacob is our stronghold.   *Selah*

ZECHARIAH 9:9–10

THE COMING OF ZION'S KING

⁹ Rejoice greatly, Daughter Zion!
Shout in triumph, Daughter Jerusalem!
Look, your King is coming to you;
he is righteous and victorious,
humble and riding on a donkey,
on a colt, the foal of a donkey.
¹⁰ I will cut off the chariot from Ephraim
and the horse from Jerusalem.
The bow of war will be removed,
and he will proclaim peace to the nations.
His dominion will extend from sea to sea,
from the Euphrates River
to the ends of the earth.

NOTES

Pause & Reflect

Here at the center of the Advent season, pause and consider what the incarnation of the Son of God means for you. Read these passages about Jesus, and use them as prompts to pray or journal through on your own, or as discussion starters for a group gathering.

For a child will be born for us,
a son will be given to us,
and the government will be on his shoulders.
He will be named
Wonderful Counselor, Mighty God,
Eternal Father, Prince of Peace.
The dominion will be vast,
and its prosperity will never end.

Isaiah 9:6–7

"For God did not send his Son into the world to condemn the world, but to save the world through him."

John 3:17

For God was pleased to have
all his fullness dwell in him,
and through him to reconcile
everything to himself,
whether things on earth or things in heaven,
by making peace
through his blood, shed on the cross.

Colossians 1:19–20

"I have come so that they may have life and have it in abundance."

John 10:10

The people walking in darkness
have seen a great light;
a light has dawned
on those living in the land of darkness.

Isaiah 9:2

He will be their peace.

Micah 5:5

HOW IS JESUS YOUR HOPE, BOTH NOW AND FOREVER?

DATE

GRACE DAY

14

Advent is a season of anticipation and celebration. The weary world rejoices at the Messiah's first advent, even as we long for His return. Use this day to pray, rest, and reflect on the hope we have because Christ left the glories of heaven to be born in Bethlehem.

The Word became flesh and dwelt among us. We observed his glory, the glory as the one and only Son from the Father, full of grace and truth.

JOHN 1:14

Homemade Sugar Scrub

DIFFICULTY ● ○ ○

CRAFT TIME
15 minutes

MATERIALS

2½ cups white sugar

¾ cup pink Himalayan salt

⅓ cup coconut oil

3 tablespoons essential oil (we used citrus)

¼ cup almond oil

DIRECTIONS

Combine sugar and salt in a mixing bowl.

In a separate bowl, melt coconut oil and mix with essential oil and almond oil. Use a whisk to combine with dry ingredients until the mixture has the consistency of sand.

Spoon into desired containers to give as gifts or for soft skin throughout the winter.

Note: This scrub is perishable. Use within 3 weeks and avoid getting excess moisture into the container to avoid mold.

. . .

The Third Sunday of Advent

DAY 15

Shepherds Sunday

Who can be astonished at anything, when he has once been
astonished at the manger and the cross? What is there wonderful
left after one has seen the Saviour? Dear reader, it may be that
from the quietness and solitariness of your life, you are scarcely
able to imitate the shepherds of Bethlehem, who told what they
had seen and heard, but you can, at least, fill up the circle of
the worshippers before the throne, by wondering at what God
has done.

Charles H. Spurgeon

LUKE 2:8-11

In the same region, shepherds were staying
out in the fields and keeping watch at night
over their flock. Then an angel of the Lord
stood before them, and the glory of the Lord
shone around them, and they were terrified.
But the angel said to them, "Don't be afraid,
for look, I proclaim to you good news of
great joy that will be for all the people:
Today in the city of David a Savior was born
for you, who is the Messiah, the Lord."

CHAINS SHALL
HE BREAK,
for the SLAVE *is*
our BROTHER,
And in HIS NAME
ALL OPPRESSION
SHALL CEASE.

The True Light

Arise, shine, for your light has come, and the glory of the LORD shines over you. ISAIAH 60:1

ISAIAH 9:2-7

[2] The people walking in darkness
have seen a great light;
a light has dawned
on those living in the land of darkness.
[3] You have enlarged the nation
and increased its joy.
The people have rejoiced before you
as they rejoice at harvest time
and as they rejoice when dividing spoils.
[4] For you have shattered their oppressive yoke
and the rod on their shoulders,
the staff of their oppressor,
just as you did on the day of Midian.
[5] For every trampling boot of battle
and the bloodied garments of war
will be burned as fuel for the fire.
[6] For a child will be born for us,
a son will be given to us,
and the government will be on his shoulders.
He will be named
Wonderful Counselor, Mighty God,
Eternal Father, Prince of Peace.
[7] The dominion will be vast,
and its prosperity will never end.

He will reign on the throne of David
and over his kingdom,
to establish and sustain it
with justice and righteousness from now on and forever.
The zeal of the LORD of Armies will accomplish this.

ISAIAH 60:1-5

THE LORD'S GLORY IN ZION

¹ Arise, shine, for your light has come,
and the glory of the LORD shines over you.
² For look, darkness will cover the earth,
and total darkness the peoples;
but the LORD will shine over you,
and his glory will appear over you.
³ Nations will come to your light,
and kings to your shining brightness.

⁴ Raise your eyes and look around:
they all gather and come to you;
your sons will come from far away,
and your daughters on the hips of nannies.
⁵ Then you will see and be radiant,
and your heart will tremble and rejoice,
because the riches of the sea will become yours
and the wealth of the nations will come to you.

JOHN 1:9-13

⁹ The true light that gives light to everyone, was coming into the world.

¹⁰ He was in the world, and the world was created through him, and yet the world did not recognize him. ¹¹ He came to his own, and his own people did not receive him. ¹² But to all who did receive him, he gave them the right to be children of God, to those who believe in his name, ¹³ who were born, not of natural descent, or of the will of the flesh, or of the will of man, but of God.

JOHN 8:12

Jesus spoke to them again: "I am the light of the world. Anyone who follows me will never walk in the darkness but will have the light of life."

REVELATION 22:1-5

THE SOURCE OF LIFE

¹ Then he showed me the river of the water of life, clear as crystal, flowing from the throne of God and of the Lamb ² down the middle of the city's main street. The tree of life was on each side of the river, bearing twelve kinds of fruit, producing its fruit every month. The leaves of the tree are for healing the nations, ³ and there will no longer be any curse. The throne of God and of the Lamb will be in the city, and his servants will worship him. ⁴ They will see his face, and his name will be on their foreheads. ⁵ Night will be no more; people will not need the light of a lamp or the light of the sun, because the Lord God will give them light, and they will reign forever and ever.

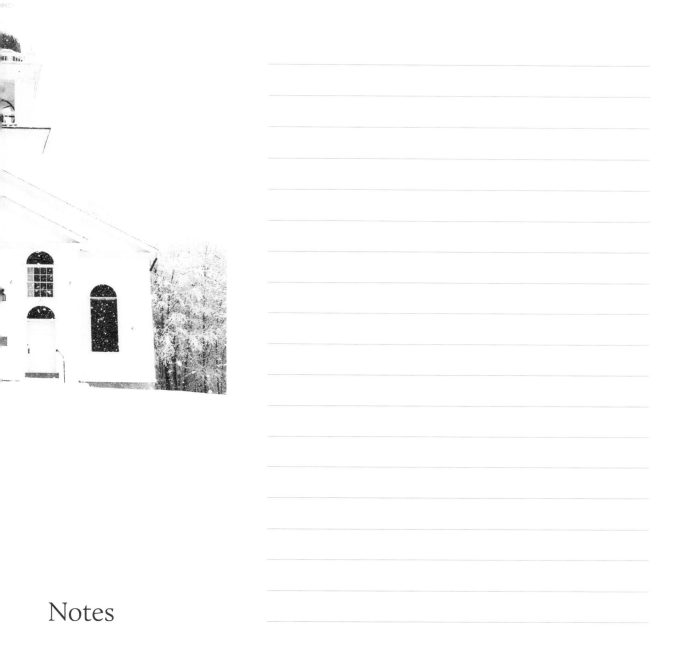

Notes

DAY

1	2	3	4	5	6	7
8	9	10	11	12	13	14
15	**16**	17	18	19	20	21
22	23	24	25	26	27	28
29	30	31				

Stained Glass Cinnamon Candy

DIFFICULTY

A Note from Raechel

This bright red science experiment is just as fun to make as it is to eat. While the mixture bubbles on the stovetop, my kids walk dutifully past the pan, shouting temperature updates from the candy thermometer. When we hit 300° on the nose, they hover closely to watch the molten sugar spread across the sheet pan as I pour. The following hour is typically characterized by questions of, "Is it cool enough to touch yet?" and, "Can I be the one to crack it this time?" It's hard to know which holiday memories will stick with them into adulthood, but I bet making cinnamon candy will be one of them.

PREP TIME
5 minutes

COOK TIME
30 minutes

SERVINGS
4 cups of candy

INGREDIENTS

2 cups white sugar

⅔ cup light corn syrup

1 cup water

¼ teaspoon oil of cinnamon

½ tablespoon red food coloring

DIRECTIONS

Combine sugar, syrup, and water in a medium saucepan.

Stir over heat until dissolved, then cook without stirring until hard-crack stage (300°F) or until brittle threads form in cold water.

Add oil of cinnamon and coloring.

Pour into shallow, buttered baking sheet. When hard, break into pieces.

The Promised Messenger

A voice of one crying out in the wilderness:
Prepare the way for the Lord. MARK 1:3

HOW DID MATTHEW AND
LUKE KNOW ABOUT THESE
EVENTS?

Being a disciple of Jesus,
Matthew could write a firsthand
account of what he witnessed.
Luke relied on what had
been written earlier and on
the eyewitness accounts of
others. But neither Matthew
nor Luke were there for the
first Christmas, so how did
they record what took place?
Zechariah and Elizabeth, being
older, surely passed away
before the Gospels were written.
The same is true for Simeon
and Anna. There's no mention
of Joseph after Jesus reached
adulthood, an indication that
he likely died while Jesus was
still young. John the Baptist
was beheaded by Herod. The
shepherds dispersed after that
divinely appointed night. And
the wise men headed back east
after their visit to Bethlehem. So
who was left to tell the story?
Mary, the mother of Jesus, "was
treasuring up all these things in
her heart" (Lk 2:19). It seems we
may have her to thank for the
Christmas story in our Bibles.

LUKE 1:5–17

GABRIEL PREDICTS JOHN'S BIRTH

⁵ In the days of King Herod of Judea, there was a priest of Abijah's division named Zechariah. His wife was from the daughters of Aaron, and her name was Elizabeth. ⁶ Both were righteous in God's sight, living without blame according to all the commands and requirements of the Lord. ⁷ But they had no children because Elizabeth could not conceive, and both of them were well along in years.

⁸ When his division was on duty and he was serving as priest before God, ⁹ it happened that he was chosen by lot, according to the custom of the priesthood, to enter the sanctuary of the Lord and burn incense. ¹⁰ At the hour of incense the whole assembly of the people was praying outside. ¹¹ An angel of the Lord appeared to him, standing to the right of the altar of incense. ¹² When Zechariah saw him, he was terrified and overcome with fear. ¹³ But the angel said to him: "Do not be afraid, Zechariah, because your prayer has been heard. Your wife Elizabeth will bear you a son, and you will name him John. ¹⁴ There will be joy and delight for you, and many will rejoice at his birth. ¹⁵ For he will be great in the sight of the Lord and will never drink wine or beer. He will be filled

with the Holy Spirit while still in his mother's womb. [16] He will turn many of the children of Israel to the Lord their God. [17] And he will go before him in the spirit and power of Elijah, to turn the hearts of fathers to their children, and the disobedient to the understanding of the righteous, to make ready for the Lord a prepared people."

MALACHI 3:1–4

[1] "See, I am going to send my messenger, and he will clear the way before me. Then the Lord you seek will suddenly come to his temple, the Messenger of the covenant you delight in—see, he is coming," says the LORD of Armies. [2] But who can endure the day of his coming? And who will be able to stand when he appears? For he will be like a refiner's fire and like launderer's bleach. [3] He will be like a refiner and purifier of silver; he will purify the sons of Levi and refine them like gold and silver. Then they will present offerings to the LORD in righteousness. [4] And the offerings of Judah and Jerusalem will please the LORD as in days of old and years gone by.

ISAIAH 40:1–5

GOD'S PEOPLE COMFORTED

[1] "Comfort, comfort my people,"
says your God.
[2] "Speak tenderly to Jerusalem,
and announce to her
that her time of forced labor is over,
her iniquity has been pardoned,
and she has received from the LORD's hand
double for all her sins."

[3] A voice of one crying out:

Prepare the way of the LORD in the wilderness;
make a straight highway for our God in the desert.
[4] Every valley will be lifted up,
and every mountain and hill will be leveled;
the uneven ground will become smooth
and the rough places, a plain.
[5] And the glory of the LORD will appear,
and all humanity together will see it,
for the mouth of the LORD has spoken.

MARK 1:1–8

THE MESSIAH'S HERALD

[1] The beginning of the gospel of Jesus Christ, the Son of God. [2] As it is written in Isaiah the prophet:

See, I am sending my messenger ahead of you;
he will prepare your way.
[3] A voice of one crying out in the wilderness:
Prepare the way for the Lord;
make his paths straight!

[4] John came baptizing in the wilderness and proclaiming a baptism of repentance for the forgiveness of sins. [5] The whole Judean countryside and all the people of Jerusalem were going out to him, and they were baptized by him in the Jordan River, confessing their sins. [6] John wore a camel-hair garment with a leather belt around his waist and ate locusts and wild honey.

[7] He proclaimed, "One who is more powerful than I am is coming after me.

I am not worthy to stoop down and untie the strap of his sandals. [8] I baptize you with water, but he will baptize you with the Holy Spirit."

Notes

1	2	3	4	5	6	7
8	9	10	11	12	13	14
15	16	**17**	18	19	20	21
22	23	24	25	26	27	28
29	30	31				

Silence and Rejoicing

You will become silent and unable to speak until the day these things take place... LUKE 1:20

LUKE 1:18-25

[18] "How can I know this?" Zechariah asked the angel. "For I am an old man, and my wife is well along in years."

[19] The angel answered him, "I am Gabriel, who stands in the presence of God, and I was sent to speak to you and tell you this good news. [20] Now listen. You will become silent and unable to speak until the day these things take place, because you did not believe my words, which will be fulfilled in their proper time."

[21] Meanwhile, the people were waiting for Zechariah, amazed that he stayed so long in the sanctuary. [22] When he did come out, he could not speak to them. Then they realized that he had seen a vision in the sanctuary. He was making signs to them and remained speechless. [23] When the days of his ministry were completed, he went back home.

[24] After these days his wife Elizabeth conceived and kept herself in seclusion for five months. She said,

[25] "The Lord has done this for me.

He has looked with favor in these days to take away my disgrace among the people."

PSALM 113

¹ Hallelujah!
Give praise, servants of the LORD;
praise the name of the LORD.
² Let the name of the LORD be blessed
both now and forever.
³ From the rising of the sun to its setting,
let the name of the LORD be praised.

⁴ The LORD is exalted above all the nations,
his glory above the heavens.

⁵ Who is like the LORD our God—
the one enthroned on high,
⁶ who stoops down to look
on the heavens and the earth?

⁷ He raises the poor from the dust
and lifts the needy from the trash heap
⁸ in order to seat them with nobles—
with the nobles of his people.
⁹ He gives the childless woman a household,
making her the joyful mother of children.
Hallelujah!

LUKE 7:18-28

¹⁸ Then John's disciples told him about all these things. So John summoned two of his disciples ¹⁹ and sent them to the Lord, asking, "Are you the one who is to come, or should we expect someone else?"

²⁰ When the men reached him, they said, "John the Baptist sent us to ask you, 'Are you the one who is to come, or should we expect someone else?'"

²¹ At that time Jesus healed many people of diseases, afflictions, and evil spirits, and he granted sight to many blind people. ²² He replied to them, "Go and report to John what you have seen and heard: The blind receive their sight, the lame walk, those with leprosy are cleansed, the deaf hear, the dead are raised, and the poor are told the good news, ²³ and blessed is the one who isn't offended by me."

²⁴ After John's messengers left, he began to speak to the crowds about John: "What did you go out into the wilderness to see? A reed swaying in the wind? ²⁵ What then did you go out to see? A man dressed in soft clothes? See, those who are splendidly dressed and live in luxury are in royal palaces. ²⁶ What then did you go out to see? A prophet? Yes, I tell you, and more than a prophet. ²⁷ This is the one about whom it is written:

See, I am sending my messenger
ahead of you;
he will prepare your way before you.

²⁸ I tell you, among those born of women no one is greater than John, but the least in the kingdom of God is greater than he."

Notes

DAY

1	2	3	4	5	6	7
8	9	10	11	12	13	14
15	16	17	**18**	19	20	21
22	23	24	25	26	27	28
29	30	31				

INGREDIENTS

5 dates

½ cup pecans

1 tablespoon shredded unsweetened coconut

1 tablespoon cacao powder

1 tablespoon coconut oil

1 tablespoon honey or agave

1 teaspoon almond extract

1 tablespoon powdered sugar

4–5 candy canes

DIRECTIONS

Start by adding dates to a bowl of water and let them soak for about an hour. Drain water and remove pit.

Place pecans in a mini food processor and pulse to break up, then tear dates into pieces and add to pecans. Pulse a few more times to incorporate.

Place mixture in a bowl and add coconut, cacao powder, coconut oil, honey or agave, and almond extract. Combine ingredients well and set aside.

Rinse food processor and wipe dry, then add powdered sugar and candy canes and pulse to create candy cane crumbs. Place in a bowl and set aside.

Using a mini ice cream scoop to measure, roll mixture into a ball, then coat well with candy cane crumbs.

Serve immediately or store in an airtight container for a day or two.

Candy Cane Date Balls

DIFFICULTY ● ○ ○

A Note from Raechel

When I think about food at Christmastime, I tend to want things that are familiar and just a little indulgent, which might explain why I was a bit skeptical about this recipe at first. *Can it really be a holiday recipe without a cup of sugar in the ingredients list?* So, I grabbed some dates and pecans and gave this recipe a shot one morning before work, and sent them to the team that same day. They were a hit! The flavors, the textures, the candy canes—they all work together to create a yummy, healthy (and yes, Christmassy!) treat.

The Annunciation

You will conceive and give birth to a son, and you will name him Jesus. LUKE 1:31

LUKE 1:26–38

GABRIEL PREDICTS JESUS'S BIRTH

26 In the sixth month, the angel Gabriel was sent by God to a town in Galilee called Nazareth, 27 to a virgin engaged to a man named Joseph, of the house of David. The virgin's name was Mary. 28 And the angel came to her and said, "Greetings, favored woman! The Lord is with you." 29 But she was deeply troubled by this statement, wondering what kind of greeting this could be. 30 Then the angel told her: "Do not be afraid, Mary, for you have found favor with God. 31 Now listen: You will conceive and give birth to a son, and you will name him Jesus. 32 He will be great and will be called the Son of the Most High, and the Lord God will give him the throne of his father David. 33 He will reign over the house of Jacob forever, and his kingdom will have no end."

34 Mary asked the angel, "How can this be, since I have not had sexual relations with a man?"

35 The angel replied to her: "The Holy Spirit will come upon you, and the power of the Most High will overshadow you. Therefore, the holy one to be born will be called the Son of God. 36 And consider your relative Elizabeth—even she has

conceived a son in her old age, and this is the sixth month for her who was called childless. ³⁷ For nothing will be impossible with God."

³⁸ "I am the Lord's servant," said Mary. "May it be done to me according to your word." Then the angel left her.

MATTHEW 1:18-25

THE NATIVITY OF THE CHRIST

¹⁸ The birth of Jesus Christ came about this way: After his mother Mary had been engaged to Joseph, it was discovered before they came together that she was pregnant from the Holy Spirit. ¹⁹ So her husband Joseph, being a righteous man, and not wanting to disgrace her publicly, decided to divorce her secretly.

²⁰ But after he had considered these things, an angel of the Lord appeared to him in a dream, saying, "Joseph, son of David, don't be afraid to take Mary as your wife, because what has been conceived in her is from the Holy Spirit.

²¹ She will give birth to a son, and you are to name him Jesus, because he will save his people from their sins."

²² Now all this took place to fulfill what was spoken by the Lord through the prophet:

²³ See, the virgin will become pregnant
and give birth to a son,
and they will name him Immanuel,

which is translated "God is with us."

²⁴ When Joseph woke up, he did as the Lord's angel had commanded him. He married her ²⁵ but did not have sexual relations with her until she gave birth to a son. And he named him Jesus.

NOTES

What Child Is This

TEXT

William C. Dix, 1865

TUNE

Traditional English Melody

*The King of kings
salvation brings; Let loving
hearts enthrone Him.*

What Child is this who, laid to rest
On Mary's lap is sleeping?
Whom angels greet with anthems sweet,
While shepherds watch are keeping?
This, this is Christ the King,
Whom shepherds guard and angels sing;
Haste, haste, to bring Him laud,
The babe, the Son of Mary.

Why lies He in such mean estate,
Where ox and ass are feeding?
Good Christian, fear, for sinners here
The silent Word is pleading.
This, this is Christ the King,
Whom shepherds guard and angels sing;
Haste, haste, to bring Him laud,
The babe, the Son of Mary.

So bring Him incense, gold, and myrrh,
Come, peasant, king to own Him;
The King of kings salvation brings;
Let loving hearts enthrone Him.
This, this is Christ, the King,
Whom shepherds guard and angels sing:
Haste, haste to bring Him laud,
The babe, the Son of Mary.

1 What child is this who, laid to rest On Mary's lap is sleep - ing?
2 Why lies He in such mean es - tate, Where ox and ass are feed - ing?
3 So bring Him in - cense, gold, and myrrh, Come pea - sant, king to own Him;

Whom an - gels greet with an - thems sweet, While shep - herds watch are keep - ing?
Good Chris - tian, fear, for sin - ners here. The si - lent Word is plead - ing.
The King of kings sal - va - tion brings, Let lo - ving hearts en - throne Him.

Chorus

This, this is Christ the King, Whom shep - herds guard and an - gels sing;

Haste, haste, to bring Him laud, The babe, the Son of Ma - ry.

The Family Line of Jesus

…and Jacob fathered Joseph the husband of Mary, who gave birth to Jesus who is called the Christ. MATTHEW 1:16

MATTHEW 1:1–17

THE GENEALOGY OF JESUS CHRIST

¹ An account of the genealogy of Jesus Christ, the Son of David, the Son of Abraham:

FROM ABRAHAM TO DAVID

² Abraham fathered Isaac,
Isaac fathered Jacob,
Jacob fathered Judah and his brothers,
³ Judah fathered Perez and Zerah by Tamar,
Perez fathered Hezron,
Hezron fathered Aram,
⁴ Aram fathered Amminadab,
Amminadab fathered Nahshon,
Nahshon fathered Salmon,
⁵ Salmon fathered Boaz by Rahab,
Boaz fathered Obed by Ruth,
Obed fathered Jesse,
⁶ and Jesse fathered King David.

FROM DAVID TO THE BABYLONIAN EXILE

David fathered Solomon by Uriah's wife,
⁷ Solomon fathered Rehoboam,
Rehoboam fathered Abijah,

WHY DOES MATTHEW BEGIN HIS GOSPEL WITH A GENEALOGY?

In ancient Israel, family records were used to track inheritance rights and claims to special offices, like the priesthood. In this genealogy, Matthew traces Jesus's lineage back to Abraham to show that Jesus is the promised descendant who will bless all the nations of the world (Gn 22:18). Along the way, Matthew includes the names of five women—Tamar (Mt 1:3), Rahab, Ruth (Mt 1:5), Bathsheba ("Uriah's wife"; Mt 1:6), and Mary (Mt 1:16). Women were not normally included in genealogies of the ancient world, and at least three of these were Gentiles, emphasizing that Jesus came for all people—male and female, Jew and Gentile alike.

Abijah fathered Asa,
[8] Asa fathered Jehoshaphat,
Jehoshaphat fathered Joram,
Joram fathered Uzziah,
[9] Uzziah fathered Jotham,
Jotham fathered Ahaz,
Ahaz fathered Hezekiah,
[10] Hezekiah fathered Manasseh,
Manasseh fathered Amon,
Amon fathered Josiah,
[11] and Josiah fathered Jeconiah and his brothers
at the time of the exile to Babylon.

FROM THE EXILE TO THE CHRIST

[12] After the exile to Babylon
Jeconiah fathered Shealtiel,
Shealtiel fathered Zerubbabel,
[13] Zerubbabel fathered Abiud,
Abiud fathered Eliakim,
Eliakim fathered Azor,
[14] Azor fathered Zadok,
Zadok fathered Achim,
Achim fathered Eliud,
[15] Eliud fathered Eleazar,
Eleazar fathered Matthan,
Matthan fathered Jacob,
[16] and Jacob fathered Joseph the husband of Mary,
who gave birth to Jesus who is called the Christ.

[17] So all the generations from Abraham to David were fourteen generations; and from David until the exile to Babylon, fourteen generations; and from the exile to Babylon until the Christ, fourteen generations.

JEREMIAH 33:19-26

[19] The word of the LORD came to Jeremiah: [20] "This is what the LORD says: If you can break my covenant with the day and my covenant with the night so that day and night cease to come at their regular time, [21] then also my covenant with my servant David may be broken. If that could happen, then he would not have a son reigning on his throne and the Levitical priests would not be my ministers. [22] Even as the stars of heaven cannot be counted, and the sand of the sea cannot be measured, so too I will make innumerable the descendants of my servant David and the Levites who minister to me."

[23] The word of the LORD came to Jeremiah: [24] "Have you not noticed what these people have said? They say, 'The LORD has rejected the two families he had chosen.' My people are treated with contempt and no longer regarded as a nation among them. [25] This is what the LORD says: If I do not keep my covenant with the day and with the night, and if I fail to establish the fixed order of heaven and earth, [26] then I might also reject the descendants of Jacob and of my servant David. That is, I would not take rulers from his descendants to rule over the descendants of Abraham, Isaac, and Jacob.

But in fact, I will restore their fortunes and have compassion on them."

ROMANS 8:15-17

[15] For you did not receive a spirit of slavery to fall back into fear. Instead, you received the Spirit of adoption, by whom we cry out, "*Abba*, Father!" [16] The Spirit himself testifies together with our spirit that we are God's children, [17] and if children, also heirs—heirs of God and coheirs with Christ—if indeed we suffer with him so that we may also be glorified with him.

Notes

DAY							
	1	2	3	4	5	6	7
	8	9	10	11	12	13	14
	15	16	17	18	19	**20**	21
	22	23	24	25	26	27	28
	29	30	31				

21

Advent is a season of anticipation and celebration. The weary world rejoices at the Messiah's first advent, even as we long for His return. Use this day to pray, rest, and reflect on the hope we have because Christ left the glories of heaven to be born in Bethlehem.

For you know the grace of our Lord Jesus Christ: Though he was rich, for your sake he became poor, so that by his poverty you might become rich.

2 CORINTHIANS 8:9

Paper Quilled Snowflake Ornament

DIFFICULTY ● ● ○

CRAFT TIME
1 hour

MATERIALS

Quilling paper (any regular paper works, too!)

Craft glue (something that dries clear)

Scissors

Needle tool or slotted quilling tool (or try a toothpick or pencil)

CUT YOUR PAPER

12 strips of ⅛ x 3¾-inch paper

6 strips of ⅛ x 7½-inch paper

6 strips of ⅛ x 15-inch paper

If you are using pre-cut quilling paper, you will use 6 uncut strips, 3 strips cut in half, and 3 strips cut into quarters.

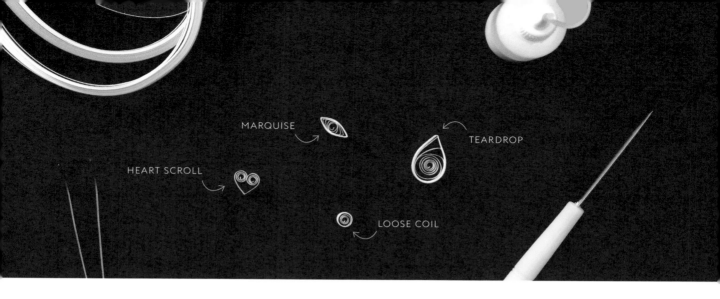

MARQUISE

HEART SCROLL

TEARDROP

LOOSE COIL

CREATE THE SHAPES

LOOSE COIL

Using one of the 3¾-inch strips, begin to roll the paper around your tool, making sure that the edges stay aligned as the paper rolls into a cylinder shape.

Carefully remove the paper from the tool, making sure to keep the edges even so they don't spiral out.

Gently let your circle unravel—it should be about 8 millimeters (or a little over ¼-inch) wide once it's unraveled.

Carefully glue the loose end of the coil to the body of the circle, creating a finished circle.

Repeat 5 more times, ending with 6 small loose coils.

MARQUISE

Using one of the 7½-inch strips, follow the same steps above to create a loose coil, noting that your unraveled coil will be slightly larger than it was for the loose coil shapes (12 millimeters or about ½-inch).

Once glued, gently pinch the coiled shape on each side of the circle to create the pointed marquise shape.

Repeat 5 more times, ending with 6 marquise shapes.

TEARDROP

Using one of the 15-inch strips, follow the same steps above to create a loose coil, noting that your unraveled coil will be about 20 millimeters or a little over ¾-inch in diameter.

Pinch one end of the glued coil to create the teardrop shape.

Repeat 5 more times, ending with 6 large teardrop shapes.

HEART SCROLL

Fold one of your 3¾-inch strips in half.

Use your tool to roll both sides of the fold inward, toward the center. No need to glue anything on this shape!

Repeat for the other 5 strips, ending with 6 heart shapes.

ASSEMBLE YOUR SNOWFLAKE

Begin by gluing your heart and marquise shapes together. Place a small drop of glue in the creased center of the heart (where you folded it in half earlier) and attach one of the pinched ends of the marquise shape there. Repeat for the other 5 sets.

Next, place a small dot of glue on the opposite pinched end of the marquise shape and attach a loose coil shape here. Try to attach the coil at the point where you glued it earlier to hide the seam. Repeat for the other 5 sets.

Now arrange your 6 teardrop shapes in a circle with the pointed ends all facing in. Glue these together to create the center ring of your snowflake.

Finally, once your teardrop ring has dried, glue the combined heart/marquise/loose coil shapes into the v-shaped spaces between the teardrop shapes.

Your snowflake is complete! Thread a string through one of the loose coils and hang on your Christmas tree, or glue your ornament to the front of a card and send to a friend.

. . .

The Fourth Sunday of Advent

DAY 22

Magi Sunday

Let us today go down to Bethlehem, and in company with wondering shepherds and adoring Magi, let us see him who was born King of the Jews, for we by faith can claim an interest in him, and can sing, "Unto us a child is born, unto us a son is given." Jesus is Jehovah incarnate, our Lord and our God, and yet our brother and friend; let us adore and admire.

Charles H. Spurgeon

When they saw the star, they were overwhelmed with joy. Entering the house, they saw the child with Mary his mother, and falling to their knees, they worshiped him. Then they opened their treasures and presented him with gifts: gold, frankincense, and myrrh.

The Magnificat

And Mary said: My soul praises the greatness of the Lord.
LUKE 1:46

LUKE 1:39-56

MARY'S VISIT TO ELIZABETH

[39] In those days Mary set out and hurried to a town in the hill country of Judah [40] where she entered Zechariah's house and greeted Elizabeth. [41] When Elizabeth heard Mary's greeting, the baby leaped inside her, and Elizabeth was filled with the Holy Spirit. [42] Then she exclaimed with a loud cry: "Blessed are you among women, and your child will be blessed! [43] How could this happen to me, that the mother of my Lord should come to me? [44] For you see, when the sound of your greeting reached my ears, the baby leaped for joy inside me. [45] Blessed is she who has believed that the Lord would fulfill what he has spoken to her!"

MARY'S PRAISE

[46] And Mary said:

My soul praises the greatness of the Lord,
[47] and my spirit rejoices in God my Savior,
[48] because he has looked with favor
on the humble condition of his servant.
Surely, from now on all generations
will call me blessed,
[49] because the Mighty One
has done great things for me,

and his name is holy.
⁵⁰ His mercy is from generation to generation
on those who fear him.
⁵¹ He has done a mighty deed with his arm;
he has scattered the proud
because of the thoughts of their hearts;
⁵² he has toppled the mighty from their thrones
and exalted the lowly.
⁵³ He has satisfied the hungry with good things
and sent the rich away empty.
⁵⁴ He has helped his servant Israel,
remembering his mercy
⁵⁵ to Abraham and his descendants forever,
just as he spoke to our ancestors.

⁵⁶ And Mary stayed with her about three months; then she
returned to her home.

PSALM 107:1-9

THANKSGIVING FOR GOD'S DELIVERANCE

¹ Give thanks to the LORD, for he is good;
his faithful love endures forever.
² Let the redeemed of the LORD proclaim
that he has redeemed them from the power of the foe
³ and has gathered them from the lands—
from the east and the west,
from the north and the south.

⁴ Some wandered in the desolate wilderness,
finding no way to a city where they could live.
⁵ They were hungry and thirsty;
their spirits failed within them.
⁶ Then they cried out to the LORD in their trouble;
he rescued them from their distress.
⁷ He led them by the right path
to go to a city where they could live.
⁸ Let them give thanks to the LORD
for his faithful love
and his wondrous works for all humanity.
⁹ For he has satisfied the thirsty
and filled the hungry with good things.

WHAT IS THE SIGNIFICANCE OF
THE SONGS IN THESE STORIES?

The four songs in the first two
chapters of the Gospel of Luke
act as a collection of hymns that
have been sung and read by the
Church during Advent for centuries.
They are commonly referred to by
their Latin names: the *Magnificat*
(Mary's song in Lk 1:46–55), the
Benedictus (Zechariah's song in Lk
1:68–79), the *Gloria in Excelsis
Deo* (the angel's song in Lk 2:14),
and the *Nunc Dimittis* (Simeon's
song in 2:29–32). Each song is an
expression of joy that God fulfilled
the promises of the Old Testament
through the arrival of our Savior.

LUKE 6:20-22

THE BEATITUDES

[20] Then looking up at his disciples, he said:

Blessed are you who are poor,
because the kingdom of God is yours.
[21] Blessed are you who are now hungry,
because you will be filled.
Blessed are you who weep now,
because you will laugh.
[22] Blessed are you when people hate you,
when they exclude you, insult you,
and slander your name as evil
because of the Son of Man.

Notes

DAY

1	2	3	4	5	6	7
8	9	10	11	12	13	14
15	16	17	18	19	20	21
22	**23**	24	25	26	27	28
29	30	31				

RECIPE

Christmas Morning Skillet

DIFFICULTY ● ○ ○

This skillet reheats well! Store leftovers in the refrigerator for an on-the-go breakfast.

PREP TIME
10 minutes

COOK TIME
50 minutes

SERVES
8

INGREDIENTS

6 eggs

2 cups shredded cheese

4-ounce can green chilis

¾ cup chopped onion

½ teaspoon salt

Hot sauce (to taste)

1–2 slices bacon, chopped (optional)

Rosemary garnish (optional)

DIRECTIONS

Preheat oven to 350°F.

Add all ingredients into a mixing bowl and combine.

Pour mixture into a buttered 8-inch cast iron skillet (or glass baking square) and bake 50–55 minutes.

Remove from oven and garnish with rosemary.

A Note from Raechel

It's possible you already have a Christmas morning breakfast tradition. But what about the day after your holiday guests arrive, or the morning you wake up in a snow-covered cabin with friends and need some easy, yummy nourishment to start the day? Consider this recipe your all-occasions skillet. It's a quick and hassle-free dish to prep, which makes it a perfect go-to when you want to feed your morning crowd something simple, substantial, and delicious.

CHRISTMAS EVE

Prepare the Way of the Lord

And you, child, will be called a prophet of the Most High, for you will go before the Lord to prepare his ways... LUKE 1:76

LUKE 1:57–80

THE BIRTH AND NAMING OF JOHN

⁵⁷ Now the time had come for Elizabeth to give birth, and she had a son. ⁵⁸ Then her neighbors and relatives heard that the Lord had shown her his great mercy, and they rejoiced with her.

⁵⁹ When they came to circumcise the child on the eighth day, they were going to name him Zechariah, after his father. ⁶⁰ But his mother responded, "No. He will be called John."

⁶¹ Then they said to her, "None of your relatives has that name." ⁶² So they motioned to his father to find out what he wanted him to be called. ⁶³ He asked for a writing tablet and wrote: "His name is John." And they were all amazed. ⁶⁴ Immediately his mouth was opened and his tongue set free, and he began to speak, praising God. ⁶⁵ Fear came on all those who lived around them, and all these things were being talked about throughout the hill country of Judea. ⁶⁶ All who heard about him took it to heart, saying, "What then will this child become?" For, indeed, the Lord's hand was with him.

⁶⁷ Then his father Zechariah was filled with the Holy Spirit and prophesied:

⁶⁸ Blessed is the Lord, the God of Israel,
because he has visited
and provided redemption for his people.
⁶⁹ He has raised up a horn of salvation for us
in the house of his servant David,
⁷⁰ just as he spoke by the mouth
of his holy prophets in ancient times;
⁷¹ salvation from our enemies
and from the hand of those who hate us.
⁷² He has dealt mercifully with our fathers
and remembered his holy covenant—
⁷³ the oath that he swore to our father Abraham.
He has given us the privilege,
⁷⁴ since we have been rescued
from the hand of our enemies,
to serve him without fear
⁷⁵ in holiness and righteousness
in his presence all our days.
⁷⁶ And you, child, will be called
a prophet of the Most High,
for you will go before the Lord
to prepare his ways,
⁷⁷ to give his people knowledge of salvation
through the forgiveness of their sins.
⁷⁸ Because of our God's merciful compassion,
the dawn from on high will visit us
⁷⁹ to shine on those who live in darkness
and the shadow of death,
to guide our feet into the way of peace.

⁸⁰ The child grew up and became spiritually strong, and he was in the wilderness until the day of his public appearance to Israel.

JOHN 1:19–23

JOHN THE BAPTIST'S TESTIMONY

¹⁹ This was John's testimony when the Jews from Jerusalem sent priests and Levites to ask him, "Who are you?"

²⁰ He didn't deny it but confessed: "I am not the Messiah."

²¹ "What then?" they asked him. "Are you Elijah?"

"I am not," he said.

"Are you the Prophet?"

"No," he answered.

²² "Who are you, then?" they asked. "We need to give an answer to those who sent us. What can you tell us about yourself?"

²³ He said, "I am a voice of one crying out in the wilderness: Make straight the way of the Lord—just as Isaiah the prophet said."

NOTES

Silent Night

TEXT

Joseph Mohr (1792-1848);
tr. John F. Young (1820-1885)

TUNE

Franz Gruber (1787-1863)

Silent night, holy night!
All is calm, all is bright
'round yon virgin mother and child;
holy infant, so tender and mild,
sleep in heavenly peace,
sleep in heavenly peace.

Silent night, holy night!
Shepherds quake at the sight,
glories stream from heaven afar,
heav'nly hosts sing alleluia;
Christ, the Savior, is born!
Christ, the Savior, is born!

Silent night, holy night!
Son of God, love's pure light,
radiant beams from Thy holy face,
with the dawn of redeeming grace,
Jesus, Lord, at Thy birth,
Jesus, Lord, at Thy birth.

Glories stream from
heaven afar, heav'nly
hosts sing alleluia.

1 Si - lent night, ho - ly night! All is calm, all is bright
2 Si - lent night, ho - ly night! Shep - herds quake at the sight,
3 Si - lent night, ho - ly night! Son of God, love's pure light,

'round yon vir - gin mo - ther and child; ho - ly in - fant, so ten - der and
glo - ries stream__ from hea - ven a - far, heaven - ly hosts__ sing al - le - lu -
ra - diant beams__ from Thy ho - ly face, with the dawn of re - deem - ing

mild, sleep in hea - ven-ly peace,___ sleep__ in hea - ven-ly peace.
ia; Christ, the Sa - vior, is born!___ Chris,__ the Sa - vior, is born!
grace, Je - sus, Lord, at Thy birth,___ Je - sus, Lord, at Thy birth.

A
Christmas Day
Invocation

Rejoice you just; it is the birthday of the Justifier. Rejoice, you who are weak and sick; it is the birthday of the Savior, the Healer. Rejoice, captives; it is the birthday of the Redeemer. Rejoice, slaves; it is the birthday of the One who makes you lords. Rejoice, free people; it is the birthday of the One who makes you free. Rejoice, all Christians, it is the birthday of Christ.

SAINT AUGUSTINE OF HIPPO

CHRISTMAS DAY

The Birth of Jesus

*Today in the city of David a Savior was born for you, who is the
Messiah, the Lord.* LUKE 2:11

LUKE 2:1-20

THE BIRTH OF JESUS

¹ In those days a decree went out from Caesar Augustus
that the whole empire should be registered. ² This first
registration took place while Quirinius was governing Syria.
³ So everyone went to be registered, each to his own town.

⁴ Joseph also went up from the town of Nazareth in Galilee,
to Judea, to the city of David, which is called Bethlehem,
because he was of the house and family line of David, ⁵ to
be registered along with Mary, who was engaged to him and
was pregnant. ⁶ While they were there, the time came for her
to give birth. ⁷ Then she gave birth to her firstborn son, and
she wrapped him tightly in cloth and laid him in a manger,
because there was no guest room available for them.

THE SHEPHERDS AND THE ANGELS

⁸ In the same region, shepherds were staying out in the fields
and keeping watch at night over their flock. ⁹ Then an angel
of the Lord stood before them, and the glory of the Lord
shone around them, and they were terrified. ¹⁰ But the angel
said to them, "Don't be afraid, for look, I proclaim to you
good news of great joy that will be for all the people: ¹¹ Today
in the city of David a Savior was born for you, who is the

WHERE DID JOSEPH AND
MARY STAY IN BETHLEHEM?

What does the word *manger* in
Luke 2:7 tell us about Mary and
Joseph's lodging in Bethlehem?
The feeding trough for animals
could have been located in
a stable or a cave used as a
stable, but the word translated
"guest room" (sometimes
translated "inn") at the end
of the verse also suggests He
could have been born in a
family home, where animals
were kept on the bottom floor.
Though the Gospel accounts
don't mention any animals,
some people believe that the
mention of a feeding trough
means animals were present
when Jesus was born.

Messiah, the Lord. [12] This will be the sign for you: You will find a baby wrapped tightly in cloth and lying in a manger."

[13] Suddenly there was a multitude of the heavenly host with the angel, praising God and saying:

> [14] Glory to God in the highest heaven,
> and peace on earth to people he favors!

[15] When the angels had left them and returned to heaven, the shepherds said to one another, "Let's go straight to Bethlehem and see what has happened, which the Lord has made known to us."

[16] They hurried off and found both Mary and Joseph, and the baby who was lying in the manger. [17] After seeing them, they reported the message they were told about this child, [18] and all who heard it were amazed at what the shepherds said to them. [19] But Mary was treasuring up all these things in her heart and meditating on them. [20] The shepherds returned, glorifying and praising God for all the things they had seen and heard, which were just as they had been told.

GALATIANS 4:1–7

[1] Now I say that as long as the heir is a child, he differs in no way from a slave, though he is the owner of everything. [2] Instead, he is under guardians and trustees until the time set by his father. [3] In the same way we also, when we were children, were in slavery under the elements of the world.

[4] When the time came to completion, God sent his Son, born of a woman, born under the law, [5] to redeem those under the law, so that we might receive adoption as sons.

[6] And because you are sons, God sent the Spirit of his Son into our hearts, crying, "*Abba*, Father!" [7] So you are no longer a slave but a son, and if a son, then God has made you an heir.

WHO WERE THE SHEPHERDS TO WHOM THE ANGELS APPEARED?

Based on their location (Lk 2:8), these shepherds might have been shepherding lambs meant for temple sacrifice. A rabbinic rule states that any animal in the fields between Jerusalem and a certain spot near Bethlehem should be presumed to be part of a temple flock. The shepherds watching over these sheep were trained to inspect newborn lambs for imperfections; only lambs that weren't injured, damaged, or blemished qualified for sacrifice. It seems appropriate, then, that the unblemished Lamb of God, who would become the ultimate sacrifice, would be announced first to these shepherds near Bethlehem.

Notes

DAY						
1	2	3	4	5	6	7
8	9	10	11	12	13	14
15	16	17	18	19	20	21
22	23	24	25	26	27	28
29	30	31				

The Travels of Mary, Joseph, and Jesus

(1) Joseph and Mary leave their home in Nazareth to register for Caesar's census in Bethlehem.

LUKE 2:1–5

(2) Mary gives birth to Jesus in Bethlehem.

LUKE 2:6–7

(3) After the forty days of purification prescribed in the law of Moses (Leviticus 12), Mary and Joseph take Jesus to Jerusalem to present Him in the temple.

LUKE 2:21–35

(4) Joseph, Mary, and baby Jesus return to Bethlehem. During this time, magi from the east come looking for the one born King of the Jews.

MATTHEW 2:1–12

(5) Joseph and Mary flee to Egypt after an angel of the Lord warns them of Herod's plan to kill Jesus.

MATTHEW 2:13–18

(6) After Herod's death, Joseph, Mary, and Jesus return to Israel to live in Nazareth.

MATTHEW 2:19–23

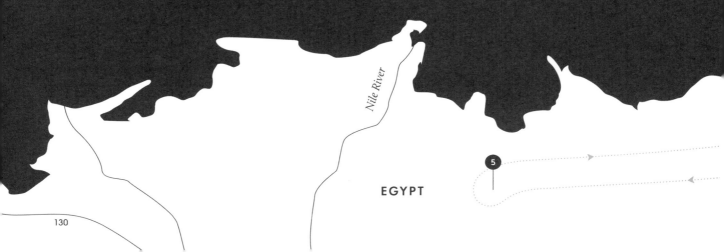

Nile River

EGYPT

(5)

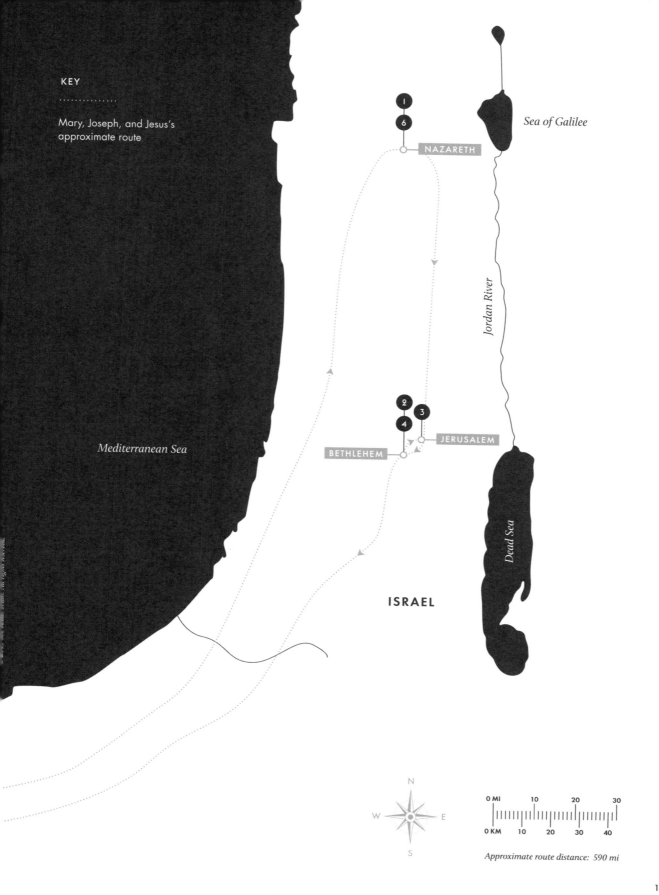

KEY

Mary, Joseph, and Jesus's
approximate route

① ⑥ NAZARETH

Sea of Galilee

Jordan River

② ③
④
BETHLEHEM JERUSALEM

Mediterranean Sea

Dead Sea

ISRAEL

N
W E
S

0 MI   10   20   30
0 KM   10   20   30   40

Approximate route distance: 590 mi

Jesus Presented in the Temple

His father and mother were amazed at what was being said about him. LUKE 2:33

LUKE 2:21-40

THE CIRCUMCISION AND PRESENTATION OF JESUS

[21] When the eight days were completed for his circumcision, he was named Jesus—the name given by the angel before he was conceived. [22] And when the days of their purification according to the law of Moses were finished, they brought him up to Jerusalem to present him to the Lord [23] (just as it is written in the law of the Lord, Every firstborn male will be dedicated to the Lord) [24] and to offer a sacrifice (according to what is stated in the law of the Lord, a pair of turtledoves or two young pigeons).

SIMEON'S PROPHETIC PRAISE

[25] There was a man in Jerusalem whose name was Simeon. This man was righteous and devout, looking forward to Israel's consolation, and the Holy Spirit was on him. [26] It had been revealed to him by the Holy Spirit that he would not see death before he saw the Lord's Messiah. [27] Guided by the Spirit, he entered the temple. When the parents brought in the child Jesus to perform for him what was customary under the law, [28] Simeon took him up in his arms, praised God, and said,

[29] Now, Master,
you can dismiss your servant in peace,
as you promised.
[30] For my eyes have seen your salvation.
[31] You have prepared it
in the presence of all peoples—

³² a light for revelation to the Gentiles
    and glory to your people Israel.

³³ His father and mother were amazed at what was being said about him. ³⁴ Then Simeon blessed them and told his mother Mary: "Indeed, this child is destined to cause the fall and rise of many in Israel and to be a sign that will be opposed— ³⁵ and a sword will pierce your own soul—that the thoughts of many hearts may be revealed."

ANNA'S TESTIMONY

³⁶ There was also a prophetess, Anna, a daughter of Phanuel, of the tribe of Asher. She was well along in years, having lived with her husband seven years after her marriage, ³⁷ and was a widow for eighty-four years. She did not leave the temple, serving God night and day with fasting and prayers. ³⁸ At that very moment, she came up and began to thank God and to speak about him to all who were looking forward to the redemption of Jerusalem.

THE FAMILY'S RETURN TO NAZARETH

³⁹ When they had completed everything according to the law of the Lord, they returned to Galilee, to their own town of Nazareth. ⁴⁰ The boy grew up and became strong, filled with wisdom, and God's grace was on him.

LEVITICUS 12:6-8

⁶ "When her days of purification are complete, whether for a son or daughter, she is to bring to the priest at the entrance to the tent of meeting a year-old male lamb for a burnt offering, and a young pigeon or a turtledove for a sin offering. ⁷ He will present them before the LORD and make atonement on her behalf; she will be clean from her discharge of blood. This is the law for a woman giving birth, whether to a male or female. ⁸ But if she doesn't have sufficient means for a sheep, she may take two turtledoves or two young pigeons, one for a burnt offering and the other for a sin offering. Then the priest will make atonement on her behalf, and she will be clean."

JOHN 19:25-27

JESUS'S PROVISION FOR HIS MOTHER

²⁵ Standing by the cross of Jesus were his mother, his mother's sister, Mary the wife of Clopas, and Mary Magdalene. ²⁶ When Jesus saw his mother and the disciple he loved standing there, he said to his mother, "Woman, here is your son." ²⁷ Then he said to the disciple, "Here is your mother." And from that hour the disciple took her into his home.

Notes

DAY

1	2	3	4	5	6	7
8	9	10	11	12	13	14
15	16	17	18	19	20	21
22	23	24	25	**26**	27	28
29	30	31				

It Came Upon the Midnight Clear

TEXT

Edmund Hamilton Sears, 1849

TUNE

Richard Storrs Willis, 1850

It came upon the midnight clear,
that glorious song of old,
from angels bending near the earth
to touch their harps of gold:
"Peace on the earth, good will to men,
from heaven's all-gracious King."
The world in solemn stillness lay,
to hear the angels sing.

Still through the cloven skies they come
with peaceful wings unfurled,
and still their heavenly music floats
o'er all the weary world;
above its sad and lowly plains,
they bend on hovering wing,
and ever o'er its Babel sounds,
the blessed angels sing.

And ye, beneath life's crushing load,
whose forms are bending low,
who toil along the climbing way
with painful steps and slow,
look now! for glad and golden hours
come swiftly on the wing.
O rest beside the weary road,
and hear the angels sing!

For lo! the days are hastening on,
by prophet seen of old,
when with the ever-circling years
shall come the time foretold
when peace shall over all the earth
its ancient splendors fling,
and the whole world send back the song
which now the angels sing.

Peace on the earth, good will to men, from heaven's all-gracious King.

1. It came up-on the mid-night clear, that glo-rious song of old,
2. Still through the clo-ven skies they come with peace-ful wings un-furled,
3. And ye, be-neath life's cru-shing load, whose forms are bend-ing low,
4. For lo! the days are has-tening on, by pro-phet seen of old,

from an-gels bend-ing near the earth to touch their harps of gold:
and still their heaven-ly mu-sic floats o'er all the wea-ry world;
who toil a-long the climb-ing way with pain-ful steps and slow,
when with the ev-er-cir-cling years shall come the time fore-told

"Peace on the earth, good will to men, from heaven's all-gra-cious King."
a-bove its sad and low-ly plains, they bend on ho-vering wing,
look now! for glad and gol-den hours come swift-ly on the wing.
when peace shall o-ver all the earth its an-cient splen-dors fling,

The world in so-lemn still-ness lay, to hear the an-gels sing.
and e-ver o'er its Ba-bel sounds, the bles-sed an-gels sing.
O rest be-side the wea-ry road, and hear the an-gels sing!
and the whole world send back the song which now the an-gels sing.

CHRIST *is the* LORD!
O PRAISE
HIS NAME FOREVER!

HIS POW'R
and
GLORY EVERMORE
PROCLAIM!

The Magi Visit the Christ Child

Falling to their knees, they worshiped him. MATTHEW 2:11

MATTHEW 2:1–23

WISE MEN VISIT THE KING

[1] After Jesus was born in Bethlehem of Judea in the days of King Herod, wise men from the east arrived in Jerusalem, [2] saying, "Where is he who has been born king of the Jews? For we saw his star at its rising and have come to worship him."

[3] When King Herod heard this, he was deeply disturbed, and all Jerusalem with him. [4] So he assembled all the chief priests and scribes of the people and asked them where the Christ would be born.

[5] "In Bethlehem of Judea," they told him, "because this is what was written by the prophet:

[6] And you, Bethlehem, in the land of Judah,
are by no means least among the rulers of Judah:
Because out of you will come a ruler
who will shepherd my people Israel."

[7] Then Herod secretly summoned the wise men and asked them the exact time the star appeared. [8] He sent them to Bethlehem and said, "Go and search carefully for the child.

HOW COULD JOSEPH AND MARY AFFORD TO FLEE TO EGYPT?

Mary and Joseph made the offering required for the poor (Lv 12:8) when they presented Jesus in the temple (Lk 2:22–23), but then fled to Egypt to escape the massacre decreed by Herod (Mt 2:13–16). This journey was incredibly costly, and it likely would not have been possible without a measure of wealth. In Mary and Joseph's case, the gifts of gold, frankincense, and myrrh from the wise men (Mt 2:11) may have funded their trip.

When you find him, report back to me so that I too can go and worship him."

⁹ After hearing the king, they went on their way. And there it was—the star they had seen at its rising. It led them until it came and stopped above the place where the child was. ¹⁰ When they saw the star, they were overwhelmed with joy. ¹¹ Entering the house, they saw the child with Mary his mother, and falling to their knees, they worshiped him. Then they opened their treasures and presented him with gifts: gold, frankincense, and myrrh. ¹² And being warned in a dream not to go back to Herod, they returned to their own country by another route.

THE FLIGHT INTO EGYPT

¹³ After they were gone, an angel of the Lord appeared to Joseph in a dream, saying, "Get up! Take the child and his mother, flee to Egypt, and stay there until I tell you. For Herod is about to search for the child to kill him." ¹⁴ So he got up, took the child and his mother during the night, and escaped to Egypt. ¹⁵ He stayed there until Herod's death, so that what was spoken by the Lord through the prophet might be fulfilled: Out of Egypt I called my Son.

THE MASSACRE OF THE INNOCENTS

¹⁶ Then Herod, when he realized that he had been outwitted by the wise men, flew into a rage. He gave orders to massacre all the boys in and around Bethlehem who were two years old and under, in keeping with the time he had learned from the wise men. ¹⁷ Then what was spoken through Jeremiah the prophet was fulfilled:

¹⁸ A voice was heard in Ramah,

> weeping, and great mourning,
> Rachel weeping for her children;
> and she refused to be consoled,
> because they are no more.

THE RETURN TO NAZARETH

¹⁹ After Herod died, an angel of the Lord appeared in a dream to Joseph in Egypt, ²⁰ saying, "Get up, take the child and his mother, and go to the land of Israel, because those who intended to kill the child are dead." ²¹ So he got up, took the child and his mother, and entered the land of Israel. ²² But when he heard that Archelaus was ruling over Judea in place of his father Herod, he was afraid to go there. And being warned in a dream, he withdrew to the region of Galilee. ²³ Then he went and settled in a town called Nazareth to fulfill what was spoken through the prophets, that he would be called a Nazarene.

JEREMIAH 31:15-17

LAMENT TURNED TO JOY

¹⁵ This is what the LORD says:

> A voice was heard in Ramah,
> a lament with bitter weeping—
> Rachel weeping for her children,
> refusing to be comforted for her children
> because they are no more.

¹⁶ This is what the LORD says:

> Keep your voice from weeping
> and your eyes from tears,
> for the reward for your work will come—
>   this is the LORD's declaration—
> and your children will return from the enemy's land.
> ¹⁷ There is hope for your future—
>   this is the LORD's declaration—
> and your children will return to their own territory.

Notes

DAY						
1	2	3	4	5	6	7
8	9	10	11	12	13	14
15	16	17	18	19	20	21
22	23	24	25	26	**27**	28
29	30	31				

THE JOURNEY OF THE WISE MEN

No one knows precisely where the wise men came from. Matthew 2:1 tells us only that they came "from the east" to worship the newborn King. Most scholars believe the wise men traveled from Mesopotamia—either Parthia or Persia—or from the Arabian peninsula. This map shows these proposed routes.

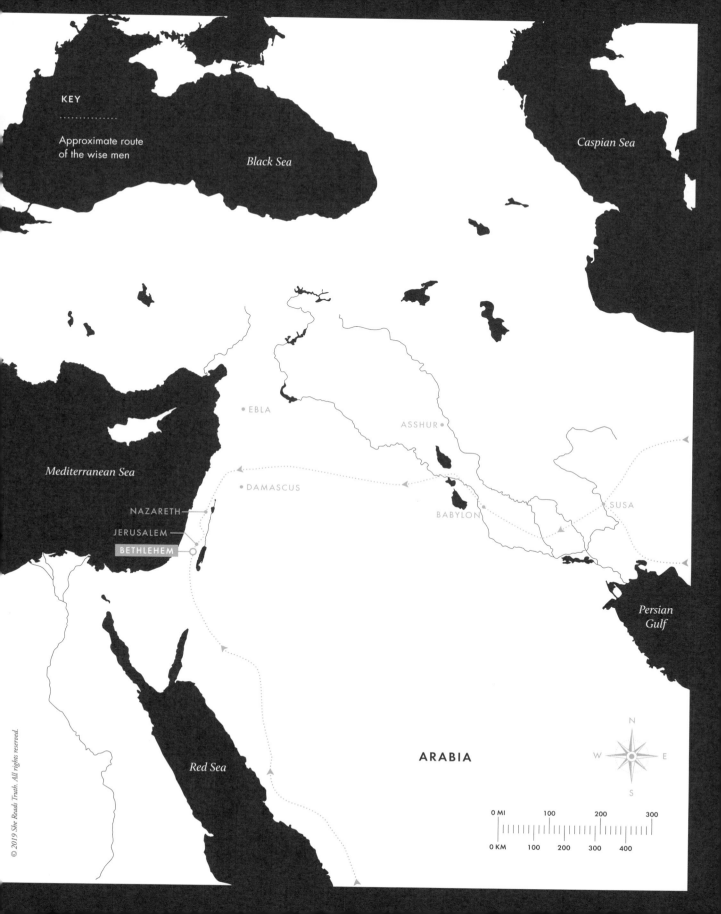

KEY

Approximate route
of the wise men

Black Sea

Caspian Sea

• EBLA

ASSHUR •

Mediterranean Sea

• DAMASCUS

BABYLON •

SUSA

NAZARETH

JERUSALEM

BETHLEHEM

*Persian
Gulf*

ARABIA

Red Sea

N
W   E
S

| 0 MI | | 100 | | 200 | | 300 |
| 0 KM | 100 | 200 | 300 | 400 | |

28

Advent is a season of anticipation and celebration. The weary world rejoices at the Messiah's first advent, even as we long for His return. Use this day to pray, rest, and reflect on the hope we have because Christ left the glories of heaven to be born in Bethlehem.

When the time came to completion, God sent his Son, born of a woman, born under the law, to redeem those under the law, so that we might receive adoption as sons.

GALATIANS 4:4–5

. . .

The First Sunday of Christmastide

DAY 29

Whether He be called the Husband of the Church, her Bridegroom, her Friend; whether He be styled the Lamb slain from the foundation of the world—the King, the Prophet, or the Priest—every title of our Master—Shiloh, Emmanuel, Wonderful, the Mighty Counsellor—every name is like the honeycomb dropping with honey, and luscious are the drops that distil from it. But if there be one name sweeter than another in the believer's ear, it is the name of Jesus. Jesus! It is the name which moves the harps of heaven to melody. Jesus! The life of all our joys. If there be one name more charming, more precious than another, it is this name. It is woven into the very warp and woof of our psalmody. Many of our hymns begin with it, and scarcely any, that are good for anything, end without it. It is the sum total of all delights. It is the music with which the bells of heaven ring; a song in a word; an ocean for comprehension, although a drop for brevity; a matchless oratorio in two syllables; a gathering up of the hallelujahs of eternity in five letters. "Jesus, I love Thy charming name, 'Tis music to mine ear."

Charles H. Spurgeon

For this reason God highly exalted him
and gave him the name
that is above every name,
so that at the name of Jesus
every knee will bow—
in heaven and on earth
and under the earth—
and every tongue will confess
that Jesus Christ is Lord,
to the glory of God the Father.

Benediction

Almighty God, who has poured upon us the new light of your Incarnate Word; Grant that the same light enkindled in our hearts may shine forth in our lives through Jesus Christ our Lord. Amen.

Book of Common Prayer

Where did I spend Christmas Day?

WHAT TIME DID I WAKE UP?

AM
———
PM

WHAT WAS THE WEATHER LIKE?

(circle one)

o

HIGH

o

LOW

WHAT MADE US LAUGH?

Who did I celebrate Christmas with?

WHAT TRADITION MEANT THE MOST TO ME THIS YEAR?

What was my favorite Christmas song this year?

TITLE

ARTIST

I LOVED GIVING

GIFT: _____

TO: _____

I LOVED RECEIVING

GIFT: _____

FROM: _____

ADVENT SCRIPTURE

_____
_____
_____
_____
_____
_____
_____
_____
_____
_____
_____
_____
_____
_____
_____

WHAT HAS GOD TAUGHT ME ABOUT HIS CHARACTER?

How did I see God
at work in 2019?

_____

_____

WHAT HAS GOD TAUGHT ME ABOUT MYSELF?

_____

_____

_____

MY FAVORITE STUDY THIS YEAR

WHAT WAS AN UNEXPECTED JOY THIS
PAST YEAR?

WHAT WAS AN UNEXPECTED SORROW?

THIS YEAR, I'M GRATEFUL FOR

THIS YEAR, I'M MOST PROUD OF

THE

most challenging

PART OF MY YEAR

THE

highlight

OF MY YEAR

My Prayer for 2020

Unwrap Beauty, Goodness, and Truth This Christmas

Reading the Bible every day can be a challenge, but She Reads Truth is here to walk alongside you each step of the way. For just $20 a month, you can get Truth delivered right to your doorstep.

AUTO-SHIP SUBSCRIBER BENEFITS:

 Each new, beautifully designed Study Book delivered right to your door

 Complimentary access to all 75+ plans on the She Reads Truth app

 Signature Auto-Ship merchandise throughout the year

 Exclusive access to community sales

 Flexible delivery options for your monthly shipment

GIVE THEM THE GIFT OF AUTO-SHIP

DIGITAL GIFT CARD

AUTO-SHIP

1 YEAR SUBSCRIPTION

AUTOSHIP.SHEREADSTRUTH.COM

Back to the
Beginning

START YOUR YEAR IN GENESIS

"In the beginning…" With that simple phrase, God invites us into the story of redemption that unfolds across all sixty-six books of the Bible. He speaks light into being, and later brings light and life to a world stumbling under the darkness of sin. He forms the first man from the dust of the earth, and then forms a nation in the womb of an elderly and barren woman.

In this five-week study, we'll journey from Eden to Egypt and come face to face with the God who has loved us since the very beginning.

Read Genesis with us, starting January 6.

Visit the shop in late November and use code BEGIN20

for 20% off your Genesis Study Book.

DOWNLOAD THE APP

STOP BY
shereadstruth.com

SHOP
shopshereadstruth.com

SEND A NOTE
hello@shereadstruth.com

SHARE
#SheReadsTruth

BIBLIOGRAPHY

France, R. T. *Matthew: An Introduction and Commentary. Vol. 1*. Tyndale New Testament Commentaries. Downers Grove, IL: InterVarsity Press, 1985.

Lueking, F. Dean. *The Grace of It All: Reflections on the Art of Ministry*. Herndon, VA: Alban Institute, 2006.

McKelvey, Douglas K., Ned Bustard, and Pete Peterson. *Every Moment Holy*. Nashville: Rabbit Room Press, 2017.

Morris, Leon. *Luke: An Introduction and Commentary. Vol. 3. Tyndale New Testament Commentaries*. Downers Grove, IL: InterVarsity Press, 1988.

Plummer, Alfred. *A Critical and Exegetical Commentary on the Gospel according to S. Luke*. International Critical Commentary. London: T&T Clark International, 1896.

Stein, Robert H. *Luke. Vol. 24. The New American Commentary*. Nashville: Broadman & Holman Publishers, 1992.

Torrey, R. A. *The New Topical Text Book: A Scripture Text Book for the Use of Ministers, Teachers, and All Christian Workers*. New, revised and enlarged edition. Chicago; New York; Toronto: Fleming H. Revell, 1897.

SHE READS TRUTH *is a worldwide community of women who read God's Word together every day.*

Founded in 2012, She Reads Truth invites women of all ages to engage with Scripture through daily reading plans, online conversation led by a vibrant community of contributors, and offline resources created at the intersection of beauty, goodness, and Truth.

. . .

**LET'S MEMORIZE
GOD'S WORD TOGETHER.**

These Scripture memory cards
correspond to the Sundays of
Advent in the **Advent 2019:
A Thrill of Hope** reading plan.

Punch out the cards and carry
them with you, place them
where you'll see them often,
or share them with a friend.

And as a bonus, we've
included four gift tags for tying
onto packages!